War, Taxation and Rebellion in Early Tudor England

By the same author

The Power of the Early Tudor Nobility: A Study of the Fourth and Fifth Earls of Shrewsbury (Harvester, 1985)

War, Taxation and Rebellion in Early Tudor England

Henry VIII, Wolsey and the
Amicable Grant of 1525

G. W. Bernard
Lecturer in History
University of Southampton

HARVESTER PRESS · SUSSEX
ST. MARTIN'S PRESS · NEW YORK

First published in Great Britain in 1986 by
THE HARVESTER PRESS LIMITED
Publisher: John Spiers
16 Ship Street, Brighton, Sussex
and in the USA by
ST. MARTIN'S PRESS, INC.
175 Fifth Avenue, New York, NY10010

British Library Cataloguing in Publication Data
Bernard, G.W.
    War, taxation and rebellion in early
    Tudor England: Henry VIII, Wolsey and the
    Amicable Grant of 1525.
    1. Forced loans —— England —— History
    —— 16th century   2. England —— Social
    conditions —— 16th century.
    I. Title
    942.05′2   HJ8047
    ISBN 0-7108-1126-8

Library of Congress Cataloging-in-Publication Data
Bernard, G.W.
    War, taxation and rebellion in early tudor England.
    Bibliography: p.
    Includes index.
    1. Great Britain—history—Henry VIII, 1509–1547.
2. Great Britain—politics and government—1509–1547.
3. Taxation—Great Britain—history—16th century.
4. Henry VIII, king of England, 1491–1547. 5. Wolsey,
Thomas, 1475?–1530. I. Title. II. Title:
Amicable grant of 1525
DA337.B47   1986   942.05′2   86-13065
ISBN 0-312-85611-3

Typeset in 11/12 point Baskerville by, Anneset,
Weston-super-Mare, Avon

Printed and bound in Great Britain by
Biddles Ltd, Guildford and King's Lynn

THE HARVESTER PRESS PUBLISHING GROUP
The Harvester Group comprises Harvester Press Ltd (chiefly publishing
literature, fiction, philosophy, psychology, and science and trade books);
Harvester Press Microform Publications Ltd (publishing in microform
previously unpublished archives, scarce printed sources, and indexes to these
collections); Wheatsheaf Books Ltd (chiefly publishing in economics,
international politics, sociology, women's studies and related social sciences);
Certain Records Ltd, and John Spiers Music Ltd (music publishing).

For Cliff, Peter, Richard and Steve,
fellow students of the 1520s

Contents

Preface

Much historical research springs from conversations and from teaching. I first thought of writing about the Amicable Grant inspired by a discussion over lunch with George Holmes, my former tutor at St Catherine's College, Oxford, on a hot July day in 1975. How was it that Henry VIII's French ambitions had been thwarted by the refusal of his subjects to finance an invasion? What comparable events had there been during the Hundred Years' War? But other commitments prevented me from pursuing these inquiries. It was not until I was asked to take over the late David Lowe's teaching at Southampton in 1980 that I considered the Amicable Grant again. One of my first students there, John Mears, chose this as the subject of his BA dissertation. The first-rate work he produced encouraged me to include this topic in my special subject teaching: I am grateful to successive generations of students for their questions and comments, especially to Alison Williams, who chose it for her assessed essay. In early 1982 I decided that the Amicable Grant was worth writing up and accordingly set about a more comprehensive reading of the sources. I remember with gratitude my colleague Alastair Duke's perceptive questioning, and encouragement, at a crucial early stage on a walk over Southampton Common after I had returned from some intensive reading in the Public Record Office and British Library. It soon became clear that the Amicable Grant was in detail more complicated than was generally recognised: the government's demands did not remain unchanged throughout.

Moreover the episode raised interesting wider questions about attitudes to warfare, about taxation and royal finance, about the relationship between Henry VIII and Wolsey, about the role of the nobility, about popular rebellion.

At another level, it raised questions about the reliability of our sources. Wherever possible I have tested one source by another. But often one is dependent on a single witness. Here my aim has been to present my evidence clearly and fully, to attend to fine detail, to consider the context in which a statement was made, to check what a man was saying against what he did. In presenting my case I have deliberately set out to answer the most ingenious counter-arguments that I can imagine and not just those actually published by other historians. If after such a process of questioning I have (especially in chapters 3, 4 and 5) arrived at the conclusion that certain key sources are best taken at face value, it is not because I have not considered more devious explanations. Trollope's Mrs Harold Smith can usefully remind us that 'we are so used to a leaven of falsehood in all we hear and say, nowadays, that nothing is more likely to deceive us than the absolute truth'. Of course it is naive *uncritically* to take evidence at face value. But it is also naive, and, what is worse, destructive, to claim that just because it is in someone's interest (as seen by us) to say something then for that reason alone it cannot be believed. I have tried to set out the difficulties, ambiguities and gaps in the evidence as I have written: it is for the reader to judge whether my interpretation rings true.

In summer 1982 Peter Gwyn, who is completing a major study of Cardinal Wolsey, urged me to go further than I had originally intended and look at the background to the foreign policy of 1525. I was quickly convinced that this was essential if I were to establish Henry's aims, and the seriousness with which he pursued them, after Pavia. The Amicable Grant itself could not be understood without some consideration of the purposes of foreign policy in the immediately preceding years. A study of that foreign policy also threw further light on the relationship between Henry VIII and Wolsey. Moreover it became clear that the nature of foreign policy significantly contributed to the outcome of the Amicable Grant. For these reasons this book begins with an assessment of war and diplomacy 1522–25.

Many friends and acquaintances passed on references and advice. Ian Archer was helpful in my pursuit of urban records as were the archivists of the many record offices to which I wrote. To Peter Gwyn I owe my knowledge of the translation of the part of Ellis Griffith's chronicle that deals with the Amicable Grant. Diarmaid MacCulloch not only drew my attention to the indictments he had discovered in the records of King's Bench but lent me his notes and card indexes. Most of my text was written in Oxford in the summer vacation 1983. During those weeks I benefited immeasurably from almost daily conversations with Cliff Davies, Steve Gunn, Richard Hoyle and Peter Gwyn, a debt which the dedication inadequately conveys. Their comments on the draft I sent out in summer 1984 were also very helpful. I am also grateful to Anthony Fletcher, Gerald Harriss, Jennifer Loach, Diarmaid MacCulloch and Greg Walker for reading and commenting upon my draft: I learned much from their comments. My colleague Brynmor Pugh gave many helpful suggestions and then most generously went out of his way to assist me as I struggled to provide late medieval comparisons (my efforts at which were also scrutinised at a late stage by Christine Carpenter and Gerald Harriss). In December 1984 I was invited to read a summary of my findings to Professor Conrad Russell's seminar at the Institute of Historical Research, University of London: I am very grateful for that opportunity and to those who asked questions on that occasion. Above all I must thank my parents for their constant support and encouragement.

G.W.B.
Southampton, February 1986

Introduction

In 1525 the subjects of Henry VIII were asked to make an 'Amicable Grant' of a substantial proportion of their wealth and income to assist the king to recover the crown of France and his rights to several French provinces. The recent capture of Francis I at Pavia made this an exceptionally favourable moment. But that request, presented by commissioners including leading noblemen and churchmen, met with refusals and a small insurrection, and was ultimately abandoned by the king. A study of the Amicable Grant is a study of Tudor government at its most ambitious and its least effective.

1

1 Foreign policy 1522–5

Does the failure of the Amicable Grant show that few Englishmen shared Henry's aspirations to French lands? How far did such aspirations influence foreign policy in the years 1522–5? And was the conduct of diplomacy itself an obstacle to decisive military action?

There was surprisingly little resistance to war against France. The most striking criticism in 1525 was that reported by Archbishop Warham from Kent in April but it should be emphasised that his letter is the only evidence of sustained opposition. 'Wher the people be commaunded to make fyers and tokens of joye for the taking of the Frenche Kinge, diuerse of thayme haue spoken that they haue more cause to wepe than to rejoyse thereat.' Several had openly wished 'that the French King wer at his libertie agayne, so as ther wer a good peace, and the Kings Grace shuld not attempte to wyne Fraunce, the wynnyng wherof shuld be more chargefull to England than profitable: and the keping therof moche more chargefull than the wynnyng'.

It shalbe the vttermust empouerisshing and vndoing of this Realme, and the greatest enriching of the Realme of Fraunce, if the Kings Grace shuld have all this money that is required and shuld spend it out of this Realme in Fraunce, wher is Grace must continually make his abode a long season, and kepe it, or else it shall be sone lost agayne. Whiche the Kings Grace long contynuaunce ther woldbe to the greate decaying and desolation of this Realme; wheras also the most parte of the nobles of this Realme must give attendaunce vpon his Grace ther, and thair spend their revenues of thair lands'.

3

Divers

'haue recomptid and repetid what infinite sommes of money the Kinges Grace hath spent alredy inuading Fraunce; ... and litle or nothing in comparation of his costes hath preuailed: in so moche that the Kings Grace at this hower hath not on fote of land more in Fraunce than his most noble father hadd, which lakked no riches or wisdom to wynne the kingdome of Fraunce if he hadd thought it expedient'.[1]

In Kent, then, some men were dismayed at the capture of Francis I, thought that any attempt to conquer France would be cripplingly expensive and feared that if it were successful it would drain England of coin. They also criticised the king for having already spent infinite sums in France with nothing to show for it. But this opposition stands virtually alone. It reads like the product of a certain war-weariness, possibly the consequence of the 'front-line' status of Kent as the point of embarkation for campaigns in France. It is altogether different from the humanist pacifism of the scholar Vives who, on hearing of Pavia, exhorted Henry VIII to magnanimity and not to pluck out one of the eyes of all Europe.[2] Moreover it was not representative. Even in Kent Warham was a little later to report that a group of refusers claimed that while they were too poor to pay what was demanded they would be ready and glad to do what their powers extended to both out of love for their king, and, significantly, 'for the respecte that they haue to the costely iourney and hiegh enterprise that is proposed in to Fraunce'.[3] Other commissioners in 1525 reported enthusiasm for, or at least acceptance of, the proposed invasion of France. The mayor and aldermen of Norwich 'considerid well that the tyme was veary commodious nowe for the king[es] highnes to invade Fraunce'.[4] The refusers at Ely 'nevertheles . . . thowght the tyme so expedyent the matter so honnorable and the consyderations laide vnto them so trewe and weyghtye that thei saide thei wold do the best thei colde' to raise money.[5] According to Edward Hall, after giving Londoners an account of the aims of the government's foreign policy in March 1525, Wolsey asked whether they thought that the king should lead an army into France: 'to the whiche many saied yea'. It is perhaps significant that it was 'many', rather than 'all' or 'a few' who assented.[6] Elsewhere there was no discussion of foreign policy and refusal to pay was usually made on the grounds of poverty rather than as dissent from the intended invasion. How far is this silence a reliable indication of attitudes to war against France? How far was it too dangerous to voice outright criticism of war against France?

Some further light may be thrown on these problems by examining attitudes in the years immediately preceding 1525. Hall, after recording Wolsey's speech to parliament in April 1523 and the subsequent debates about taxation, suggests general, if perhaps somewhat reluctant, acquiescence: 'it was concluded, that the kyng of necessitie, muste nedes make strong warre on the realme of Fraunce', for which the duke of Suffolk had been appointed lieutenant.[7] In Ellis Griffith's chronicle, the 1523 campaign appears, in effect, as a 'class war' for the benefit of king, noblemen, gentlemen and professionals only. Royal instructions to Suffolk to remain in France over the winter were 'well received by the gentlemen of England and those men of the common soldiers who had set their minds on being men of war'.[8] Military campaigns offered opportunities for profit. Frenchmen could be taken prisoner, as they were at Belle Castle and near Montdidier, and perhaps be lucratively ransomed. Captured towns like Montdidier could be looted: not only wine but also honey, salt, featherbeds, nappery, coverings, household stuff, leather, pieces of pewter.[9] War also offered the chance of social promotion: the duke of Suffolk created sixteen knights in November 1523, including Edward Seymour and John Dudley, the future rulers of England in the reign of Edward VI.[10] But for most, war was unpleasant, as Griffiths noted. 'Those who were thinking of their wives and children and husbandry and those cowardly men with base hearts who would rather go home to their mothers and fathers, some to plough and thresh, others to follow the cart and hedge and dig and live niggardly, these were unwilling and were angry with anyone who talked about staying there during the winter.' Such men were lazy in lighting fires and making huts to keep themselves dry and warm. They took part in a near-mutiny, shouting 'home, home!', which turned an orderly retreat into a fiasco.[11] But how representative of wider attitudes were the discontents of soldiers during a difficult campaign?

There is some evidence of reluctance in 1524. In March, Louis de Praet, Charles V's ambassador, thought English lords much inclined to peace or to a truce.[12] Because of the coming of an ambassador from the pope in April, 'men hoped that peace should ensue', wrote Hall.[13] On the other hand, Hall also tells us how at Christmas, one of the visiting Scots negotiators asked an English gentleman whether the king and his lords were as merry in wartime as they were then: yes, replied the gentleman, adding 'for the kyng of England maie sit in his chaire and dammage the French kyng for the Lordes and cominaltie of England praie for the continuaunce of warre, for by the warres of Fraunce they wynne, and lose not'.[14] It is important not to confuse hopes and inclinations for peace with preferences for or objections to particular alliances. In summer 1524, Hall informs us, the king appealed to divers lords and gentlemen to make preparations in case he or his lieutenant took advantage of the rebellion of the duke of Bourbon to invade France. Everyone duly got ready, but 'the people murmured and saied, that it were much better, that the kyng should maintein his warres, with his owne subiectes, and spend his treasure on them, then to trust the Duke of Bourbon'. What is being criticised here is not war against France but support of Bourbon.[15] There were some who, while not pacifists, gave priority to Scottish affairs,[16] even to the point of raising fundamental objections to any campaign in France. That was the burden of an anonymous draft of a speech intended for delivery in the 1523 parliament. It was too dangerous for the king to go over in person. Great difficulties had been experienced in victualling forces sent across in earlier expeditions: any thrust deep into France would expose English lines of communication as cruelly vulnerable to attack. Vast sums had been spent on such campaigns: 'the wynnyng of Tyrouen ... cost ... more than xx^{ti} suche vngracious Dogholes cowld be worth'. 'Who entendyth Fraunce to wyn with Skotland let hym begyn.'[17] Others — according to Hall, 'all the people of Englande' — by early 1525 so grudged against the Netherlanders for giving so little assistance that 'it was thought surely that the kyng of England, would haue had peace with the French kyng' if the battle of Pavia had not intervened. Different again were those who favoured the French, though possibly they did so primarily out of self-interest. Hall describes how Joachim, the agent of Louise of Savoy, the French king's mother, 'offered pencions to diuerse young men aboute the kyng, of the which some were very glad, and so the noyse by reson of suche offers ran, that a peace was likely to ensue in shorte space'.[18]

The variety of attitudes which such limited and scrappy evidence reveals was a result of the fluidity of foreign policy. Anglo-French rivalry, while traditional, was nevertheless not bitterly ideological, nor, in the 1520s, set fast by the memory of any recent outrages or defeats that demanded to be avenged. Indeed in 1514, in 1518, and as recently as 1520, friendship between the English and French monarchies had been extravagantly celebrated. In 1521, however, changing perceptions by Henry VIII and Wolsey of relations between the emperor and the king of France led at the conference of Bruges to a secret English alliance with Charles V against Francis. It would be made public by March 1523 and lead to a 'great enterprise', a joint attack against the French.

The king's honour, as Peter Gwyn has shown, was the mainspring of English diplomacy: united action offered 'a golden opportunity to win honour and glory'.[19] References to honour were a feature of justifications of war. Francis had broken his promises so often 'that the kyng of his honor could no longer suffre'.[20] Wars were still, in the early sixteenth century, the sport of kings, noblemen and courtiers, a continuation of the world of chivalry, of jousts and tournaments, that offered, as we have seen, opportunities for profit and prestige. Human costs, especially loss of life or injuries to civilians, and damage to their property and livelihoods, were not highly valued.

Yet if honour was the ultimate prize, nevertheless diplomacy and military action were never just a game but were rather undertaken seriously. There were real fears, at times, of diplomatic isolation and of consequent bad deals from other rulers in the myriad disputes, large and small, that never disappeared; fears, also, of invasion by the Scots across the northern borders, and fears of raids by the French along the south and east coasts, none of them empty or implausible concerns.[21]

A dynastic challenge to Henry VIII was remote but still thinkable. Richard de la Pole, one of seven sons of John duke of Suffolk (†1491) and Elizabeth, Edward IV's sister, called himself duke of Suffolk and White Rose after his elder brother Edmund had been executed in 1513 and then laid claim to the crown of England. In exile since 1501, he had been taken up by Louis XII of France in 1512–13 and later lived as a pensioner first of Louis and then of Francis I, in Metz, and afterwards in Toul. In the early 1520s Francis made greater use of his services. From 1520 there were rumours that he would be sent to Scotland;[22] in late 1522 he was with Francis in Paris and in 1523 it was planned first that both the duke of Albany (the French-born heir presumptive to Scotland) and de la Pole should go to Scotland to lead an invasion of England, and then that Albany should go first (which he did) while de la Pole should look for a suitable moment to land directly in England, an opportunity which, in the event, never came.[23] In spring 1524 he was serving in French forces on the borders with Flanders, leading a contingent of German mercenaries;[24] in February 1525 he was killed at the battle of Pavia.[25]

From time to time there are hints that he had some support in England. Perhaps it was for correspondence with him or his agents seen as treasonable that Geoffrey Blythe, bishop of Coventry and Lichfield, was briefly imprisoned, although other explanations are possible.[26] An official memorandum examining what had to be considered if the king were to invade France noted that de la Pole claimed that he had plenty of friends in England who, however, would not dare declare themselves until he appeared. He also counted on many in Ireland.[27] One John Goghe of Lancashire confessed that he had spoken with de la Pole in Rouen;[28] two men, Nicholas Friske and John Asome, had tried to recruit one Aleyn Dawse of East Dereham to join de la Pole's 'harness';[29] one Simon Jones confessed in early 1523 that de la Pole had sent him to the Netherlands to find out Henry's and the emperor's military intentions and then to England to inquire who was of de la Pole's party, and, in particular, to tell Lords Derby and Stafford (the latter of whom might have been supposed to hold a grudge against Henry for the execution of his father in 1521) his mind;[30] a spy sent by de la Pole was taken in the Netherlands in April 1524; two London apprentices went to Rouen to seek the service of de la Pole.[31] It was to those regions where the late duke of Buckingham had held lands that Francis was intending to send de la Pole in June 1522: a further sign that de la Pole and Francis hoped to draw on any resentment felt by Buckingham's heir, Lord Stafford, at his father's recent downfall.[32] Of course none of this amounted to very much. In outlining the threats to the king from Francis in early 1523, Wolsey, both when writing to Sampson, and when making a case in parliament, emphasised that from Albany but never mentioned de la Pole.[33] Henry and Wolsey were on their guard but were never seriously troubled. Yet small as it was, the potential challenge from de la Pole, and its possible exploitation by Francis I, in what might have become a repetition of the events of the mid-1480s in which the French helped an earlier English usurper, Henry VIII's father Henry Tudor, against Richard III, show that the substance of foreign policy mattered. The dangers posed by the French were real and taken seriously. No doubt surviving position papers distort — imperial ambassadors are likely to write at length about diplomatic negotiations, Henry's and Wolsey's letters to their agents overseas survive abundantly — yet even Hall's *Chronicle* conveys the importance of relations with other rulers, giving lengthy and detailed accounts of the campaign of 1523 and even of the skirmishes of 1524. It is hard to see why the overriding impression obtained from a reading of the *Calendar of State Papers, Spanish,* that diplomacy absorbed much of the energies of Henry and Wolsey, should be false.

At first sight, the themes of English foreign policy from late 1521 to 1525 were that Charles V was England's ally, Francis I England's enemy and that legitimate English claims in France would be pursued by force. Yet matters never remained clear-cut for long. If honour was the aim, then honour might perhaps be better obtained by an honourable peace rather than by a disastrous, and therefore dishonourable, military campaign. If security was the goal, then a peace or a truce could offer at least short-run guarantees. Thus if in these years Henry was keen on an invasion of France, he was only willing to do so given full support by Charles V — which meant, above all, men and supplies from the Netherlands, since the English could not supply all their own military and material needs. He was reluctant throughout, however, to stage on his own, or with limited assistance, a costly raid into France that would bring him little but by distracting the French would greatly aid the emperor's campaigns against the French in Italy. English suspicions of the imperialists could often flare up into angry reproaches. There were always differences of priorities, of tactics: should an invasion be attempted now or next year, should it be into Picardy or Normandy, or should Scotland be dealt with first, and so on. Moreover if Henry saw Francis as his enemy, nonetheless the threat that the French posed because of their alliance with the Scots, and especially by their patronage of the duke of Albany, meant that Henry might listen to French offers of a deal, the more so when the terms proposed were generous. Much depended on finance, as we shall see. Diplomatic stances were greatly influenced by events elsewhere. How was Charles faring in his wars against the French in Italy? If he was doing well, that might be a case for strengthening the alliance; if, on the contrary, the French were winning, that was a time for delay, and, possibly, for dealings with the French as a form of insurance. Decisions of this kind had to be made on imperfect information, and, of course, on intelligent guesses about who would do best next. English foreign policy in these years was thus highly opportunistic, in turn cautious and aggressive. It was by no means predictable. On learning of Pavia, John Lord Berners at Calais asked for instructions on whether to celebrate Charles V's victory: they were doing so in Flanders but he would do nothing until he heard the king's pleasure. English foreign policy had become so variable that even its executants could not safely decide how to respond to a great event.[34] This makes seeking out general attitudes to France especially difficult: comments by Henry and Wolsey, reported by the imperial ambassadors, must always be tested for bluff and set in the context of current negotiations. When, for example, Wolsey is raising difficulties about agreeing to a demand made by the imperialists, is he just increasing his demands to extract a better deal?[35] It is quite improper to use such comments to conclude, for example, that 'it was known that Wolsey had quite deserted the imperial cause, and that he was discussing with France and the imperial powers the means of resistance to the emperor's menacing authority'.[36] It is misleading to write the history of foreign policy in terms of long-run, full alliances between one country and another, which then switch into similar long-run alliances with another country. The reality was much more subtle, preferences were less deep, and all was influenced by the need for insurance, by the logic of military events, by suspicions of deception and by the deception of others. But this fluidity of policy — when attitudes could oscillate in days, as in summer 1524, from warm negotiations with the French to preparations for an invasion — had its effects on what could be achieved. If alliances were so tenuous, if intentions could change so easily, if a key principle was to keep all options open, it would be hard work indeed to rally opinion when it was officially determined to take decisive action, for example to launch an invasion. The propaganda campaigns against the French in 1523 and 1525 were much too *ad hoc*, somewhat defensive, with an air of protesting too much. The list of lapses by Francis seems as much the basis for a deal as a justification of war. The fluidity of alliances played its part in the failure of the government to secure the financial support of the country for an invasion of France in 1525. The projected campaign that year was not the culmination of a sustained process but the sudden (and, as we shall see, by no means unambiguous) response to a single event.

An earlier development, the treachery of the duke of Bourbon in France, similarly shifted the balance of policy in favour of aggression. Charles V had been keen on an English invasion of France in early 1523, assuring the English ambassadors, Boleyn and Sampson, that he would be ready, urging Henry to invade Guyenne, and writing to his ambassadors in England of the importance of waging war that summer.[37] The English had been more cautious. Boleyn and Sampson wrote from Spain, suspicious of Charles' intentions: he was poor, his main interests were in Italy and he complained that Henry was using their alliance for his private profit against the Scots.[38] Henry and Wolsey continued to give de Praet, Charles' ambassador, grounds for mistrust during negotiations in May.[39] Both sides clearly felt that the other was reaping the main benefit of their alliance.

But the appeal from the would-be rebel Bourbon changed the situation. Although only a little earlier Henry and Wolsey had despaired of him,[40] news that he had sent the sieur de la Motte secretly to Margaret in the Netherlands, that is, that he was making contact with Charles V, led to a resolution by the council (with the duke of Suffolk, the earl of Shrewsbury, Sir Robert Wingfield and three bishops present) that the English would invade France with a force of 15,000 under Suffolk in the late summer, with the aim of capturing Boulogne.[41] The prospect of substantial support from one of the most powerful of French noblemen transformed English perceptions. Charles, duke of Bourbon (1490–1527), one of the greatest noblemen in France, who held 'an unusually compact block of territory in central France', had been provoked by the seizure of his dead wife's lands by the Queen mother, Louise of Savoy, into dabbling in treason with Charles V. If he were to turn this into outright rebellion against Francis I, he might be able to offer the English assistance on a scale comparable to that given to Henry V by the duke of Burgundy between 1414 and 1416.[42] A treaty between Henry and Charles was concluded on 2 July. By mid-August Henry was to send an army of 15,000 into France; Margaret would supply 3,000 horse and 3,000 foot from the Netherlands; and Charles would send 20,000 men into Guyenne. A formal tripartite league, including Bourbon, was drawn up on 4 August.[43]

Even so, there were doubts and divisions from the start. On 3 July Wolsey wrote to Sampson and Jerningham, ambassadors with Charles V, that 'there is not like to growe so grete benefit or commodite therof as was estemed'.[44] He was still doubtful about Bourbon on 9 August.[45] Bourbon himself refused to acknowledge Henry as king of France and the question was referred to Charles for later adjudication.[46] Meanwhile as the duke of Suffolk was preparing to go over to France there were large divisions between Charles and Henry about the strategy he should employ. Henry was thinking of a siege of Boulogne; Charles clearly preferred English forces to sweep into the heart of France.[47] Wolsey neatly stated English fears in July. It was essential that Henry and Charles attack Francis properly and avoid the waste of half-hearted, small-scale raids.

For better it shalbe oons to annoye the common enemye with grete puissances, which he shold not be able to resiste, wherby he may be dryven to offre and comme unto reasonable and honourable condicions, then this in dryving the tyme litel and litel to wast and consume treasour. . . . For by suche drybbing warre, as hit hitherto hathe ben made by the said princes, the common enemye is rather exalted.[48]

News from Bourbon in early-to-mid September first persuaded Wolsey to press for an aggressive policy and swallow his earlier doubts, and then persuaded Henry to give up the siege of Boulogne in favour of an invasion deep into France. A key event here was the return from Bourbon of Sir John Russell who reported enthusiastically to Wolsey and to the king.[49] At this time Floris van Egmont, graaf de Buren, the commander of the Netherlands forces, similarly appealed to Wolsey.[50] Wolsey was evidently convinced and wrote to Henry, who was at Abingdon, urging him to give up the idea of taking Boulogne and instead to send his army to places suggested by Bourbon which, he had been informed, might easily be taken, seeing 'great apparence of wynnyng some greate parte of France, or at the lest wise all that is in this side the water of Some'. This, Wolsey added, would be honourable and beneficial to the king, and also more defensible than all of Normandy, Gascony and Guyenne. Henry was much more doubtful and made objections which the outturn of the campaign showed to be all too accurate. It was late in the year. It would be hard to capture several of the places aimed at. Above all victualling an army would be difficult. True, the 'slaknes of the Burgonyons provision' — a revealing example of Henry's mistrust of his allies — made the chances of a successful siege of Boulogne small yet he feared that marching forward would produce 'little profite with more charge, dayngr, and perel'. Because of the time of year, and likely 'wete wether, and rotten ways', this would be 'more incommodiouse' to men's feet 'they should some tyme lye still, and some tyme march' than if they only stayed in one place. Especially, Henry thought, 'the wetenes of the cuntre, upon the rivers side, shall not suffre his army to march with artillery, either groce inough for batery, or sufficient for the feld', without which they would be unsafe. He did not think that Corbie, Compiègne and other towns on the Seine were so easily to be taken as some claimed, reminding Wolsey of what had happened at Hesdin the previous year. But 'if the townys be so easy to be wonne, as the Burgonyons and other make hit . . . than . . . after his army withdrawen and discharged, they wilbe as easy to be loste', particularly if Francis were to attack them with a strong force. 'It were not so myche honour shortely to wynne theym, as hit wold be dishonour shortely to lose theym'. If, moreover, towns like Thérouanne, Boulogne and Montreuil were left behind untaken, it was most unlikely that they would easily be starved into surrender and their garrisons would jeopardise the supply of victuals to the invaders. This was in any case a serious worry. 'If they shuld marche far, ther wold be great difficultie in the vitailling'. There was an acute shortage of carts. Moreover if the army behaved as an army of conquest rather than as raiders, proclaiming liberty and sparing the country from burning and spoil, that would be demoralising for the men. 'The bare hope' of booty, 'though they gate litle', was a great encouragement to men marching 'in hard wether, with many sore and grevous incommoditees'. They would have 'evill will to march far forward', thought Henry, 'and theyre capitayns shall have myche adoo to kepe theyme from crying Home! Home!'.[51] Despite these weighty and prophetic arguments, after much persuasion Wolsey and Russell prevailed: the duke of Suffolk did not besiege Boulogne but rather launched an invasion into France together with the Netherlanders under Buren in support of Bourbon's rebellion and Henry's claims.[52]

The purpose of the campaign was to seize several French towns, perhaps to fortify one or two, or establish them as bases for supplies, and then to meet up with the duke of Bourbon's forces in Bourbon's 'country', to the east of Paris, to attack the French capital, in the hope that by then Bourbon's rebellion would have spread further.[53] At first all went well. 'Ther shalbe never such or like opportunite geven hereafter for the atteynyng of Fraunce', wrote Wolsey on 3 November.[54] Suffolk's and Buren's forces advanced from late September via, notably,

Coquelles (19 September), Ardes (29 September), Belle Castle, Esquerdes, Cordes (1 October), Ancre, Bray (20 October) on the river Somme, which was to be a staple for victuals, and then Montdidier (70 miles from Paris) which was taken on 27–28 October.[55] That was the high point of the campaign. There were hopes of going on to Noyon, Compiègne, Sens and as far as possible towards Paris.[56] But all was not as well as it seemed. There had been difficulties among Suffolk's forces at the start. Welsh soldiers had begun the campaign by rioting in Calais.[57] At St Omer 'many a man was unwilling to go further because the weather was wet and winter was beginning to show his face'. At Bray many complained because they had water in their boots and said they would retreat.[58] The gentlemen leading the army disagreed on whether to cross the Somme: 'diuerse souldiers' agreed with those who were unwilling because it would put them out of reach of victuals. It took Sandys' courageous example to get men to follow.[59] By this time disease and desertion had 'sore diminished' the army.[60] After the capture of Montdidier, the Burgundians and the English began 'to waxe wery' 'for euery day was foule wether and raine both day and night'. 'Wherfore dyuers companies fell to grudgyng saiyng, now you may see that by our remouyng we shall be ledde from place to place all this wynter, whiche is to the vtter losse of our lyues'.[61] Suffolk had a council to decide what to do. He had not half enough people to hold the towns they had captured, nor one tenth of the artillery and ordnance needed fully to man one of them.[62] There was also 'contrariete in opynyons' between Suffolk and Buren.[63] The Burgundians were treating the campaign as an occasion for looting, and then deserting.[64] Buren was not receiving any money from the Netherlands: by 23 October his finances were so desperate that he asked Henry to support his troops.[65] A contingent of German mercenaries was just pillaging.[66] Worse still, Bourbon let Henry down. He failed to lead a rebellion and he failed to raise any forces to meet up with Suffolk and Buren: above all, he fled from Champagne to the safety of Besançon and then Italy.[67]

Henry had been planning that his army should winter in France.[68] On hearing from Sandys, sent by Suffolk in early November to report the position and to ask for further instructions, Henry decided to appoint William Blount, fourth Lord Mountjoy, an experienced military commander, to lead an army of 6,000 to relieve and reinforce Suffolk, 'for we will in no wise that the army shall break'. The relief army was indeed raised but it was too late.[69] Meanwhile, anxious about their lines of supply, Suffolk and Buren had decided to recross the Somme and take Bohain and Guyse, awaiting reinforcements, rather than overwintering at Montdidier, Bray and Ancre.[70] But at this point weather conditions deteriorated: great winds and rain were followed by 'fervent frost' 'so sore that many a souldier dyed for colde, some lost fyngers, and some toes, but many lost their nailes of their handes, whiche was to them a great grefe'. Many died.[71] Mutiny among the English forces increased: it was 'no worse being hanged in England than dying of cold in France'. One soldier complained that 'if I had known at the beginning of the night that there would be as much frost and snow as this I would not have taken so much trouble to search my shirt for lice, but I could have hung it out in the wind and let them die of cold, as we shall do if we stay here any longer'. Next morning 'they began to talk about their journey to England all through the host and then they shouted out loud, 'Home! Home!'[72] Suffolk and the captains were compelled to yield to the inevitable: by mid-November, the army was in retreat, the campaign over.[73] When Suffolk attempted to rally his men he could get scarcely one quarter; 'souldiers dyed . . . vittail failed . . . of truth the souldiers would not abide'.[74] It was reported to Lord Clifford in early December that 'the soldiers beyond the sea comes a pace against theire captaines wills . . .'.[75] As Wolsey was to put it to Sampson in Spain, Henry wanted his army to overwinter in France but in vain

as the season of the yere was so fervent in extreme coldes, and other sore wedders, that neither men ne beestes could lenger endure marching in the felde, but died dailly and nightly on bothe parties in great nombers for colde, and diverse other lost thair fyngers, handes and fete, being frosen and dede upon thair bodyes and sens dailly cut of.[76]

The campaign did nothing to make Henry and Wolsey feel more sympathetic towards Charles, Margaret and the Burgundians. In mid-November Buren had led the

Burgundians back to Valenciennes, partly no doubt (as Margaret claimed) because of the weather, but more (as the English alleged) because they had not been paid (allegations that are convincing given Buren's appeal to Henry for money in late October and the evidence of Buren's repeated but unsuccessful requests to Margaret for money). Margaret's request that the English should finance these forces from 1 December was not well received.[77] By now there was a long history of the failure of the Netherlanders to meet their promises of supplies and military assistance. This had already caused difficulties in the campaign of 1522. The earl of Surrey had then complained to Wolsey in September that if they had not been better supplied with beer from England and Calais than from the Netherlands, they should long ago have been compelled to leave the field.[78] Wolsey in the same month had threatened the emperor's ambassador that Henry would withdraw his army if a remedy for the lack of victual and powder were not found.[79] That such complaints were well-founded was admitted by the imperial ambassadors in a letter they wrote to Charles in August.[80] The difficulty, as Wingfield noted, was the weakness of central authority in the Netherlands: 'the folks of this country seem rather to be lords than subjects'.[81] Not surprisingly, some consequent wariness was present in the negotiations that led up to the 1523 campaign. There were quarrels over the numbers of horse and foot that Margaret was to provide and over payments to German mercenaries, complaints that agreed contingents did not arrive, reproaches over the lack of carts and draught horses.[82] During the campaign Wolsey frequently spoke in anger to the imperial ambassador. By 29 October he was in a great rage, complaining of the great expense to which Henry had gone and how little the emperor had done.[83] So annoyed was he a little later that he told de Praet that if Charles and Margaret intended to throw all the burdens on the king, then it would be better for the kingdom to be at war with Charles than with the French.[84] In December de Praet reported Henry's and Wolsey's great annoyance at Margaret's failure to finance her forces under Buren.[85] In January 1524 Knight, writing from the Netherlands, suggested that if Henry's army were to cross over that year they would do better alone than joined with the

Burgundians.[86] Reports came that the Netherlanders' main preoccupations were in Gelders and Friesland and (from Sampson and Jerningham in Spain) that the emperor was too poor to help himself or his friends. When his army would be ready, God knew; his advisers' only object was peace. Charles would never, Sampson deduced, wish to extend Henry's dominions, or to keep soldiers in the field a day longer than suited his own purposes.[87] De Praet wrote in late January how Henry and Wolsey were marvellously bitter, full of reproaches, threatening to leave the alliance and to tear up the treaties between them and the emperor. They had just heard from Sampson and Jerningham how little effort Charles was making. Wolsey continued to blame Margaret. De Praet more or less endorsed these complaints as well-founded when he urged Charles not to agree to anything he could not fulfil.[88] Sampson and Jerningham again wrote that they saw no intention on the emperor's part to extend Henry's dominions or to see him as king of France.[89] Throughout 1524 Sampson sent despatches emphasising Charles' poverty and consequent inability to offer worthwhile assistance to Henry.[90] Meanwhile Wolsey suspected that one of Margaret's counsellors in the Netherlands, the Provost of Utrecht, was a secret supporter of the French.[91] It is not surprising that Wolsey wrote that 'the charges, labour, travaile and studye' of the king in these wars 'hathe tended only to the Emperours avauntage'.[92]

Against this background of mistrust, broken promises and abortive campaigns, Henry and Wolsey had to decide what to do in 1524. According to de Praet, Henry was keen to invade France again: having seen how so small a force had been able to cross the Somme the previous year, he now firmly believed that he could conquer all the frontier provinces and even Paris.[93] But if this remained Henry's aim, it was cautiously and conditionally pursued. Throughout 1524 Charles was very keen that the English should make a further invasion of France. Embroiled in a difficult campaign in Italy, the imperialists hoped to benefit from any diversion that the English could stage in northern France (or indeed Guyenne). Charles' and de Praet's letters show the emperor's constant encouragement of Henry and Wolsey to prepare for such an invasion. On 31 March Charles instructed de Praet to say he was willing to assist an English invasion of Picardy from the Netherlands;[94] on 15 April de Praet was told to say that he wished to exert all his power to aid Henry's proposals for war, even promising 3,000 horse and 3,000 foot from the Netherlands, which Margaret was ordered to supply.[95] Do all you can, urged Charles on 21 April, to hasten the descent of the army into France so that the favourable season were not lost.[96] 'Car si je suis prospère, ou si j'ay infortune en Italie', he wrote to Margaret, 'tousiours me vient il a poinct que lesdits anglois soient aux champs ceste année': earlier he had encouraged her to stretch her credit as far as possible to finance a joint campaign.[97] In late May Charles sent a gentleman of his bedchamber, de Courrières, to beg Henry to invade.[98] Bourbon's agent urged Henry on. There had never been a better opportunity: the time would come when Henry would assume his rightful crown.[99] It was foolish, wrote Charles, to wait for a 'great enterprise' in 1525: there was a good opportunity now.[100] To such clamorous encouragement Henry and Wolsey responded with mitigated enthusiasm. They insisted that any venture should be properly supported. Charles was to pay for cavalry and infantry from Flanders. There had to be clear signs of military preparedness. Charles was to place an army in the field from Spain.[101] Much of this reluctance may have been bluff, designed to raise the terms offered by an importunate ally. But in the light of the campaign of 1523 Henry and Wolsey were understandably wary.[102]

One question that troubled the English was just how strong the French were. It would be unwise to take them on if they were proving overwhelmingly successful in Italy. Even at his keenest on an invasion, Henry, as reported to de Praet, believed that only if Charles was victorious in Italy would he have an excellent opportunity to achieve something substantial. In March Wolsey said that Henry was unwilling to decide on an invasion until he saw whether the French could be driven out of Italy. It seemed to him that their army was as strong as the emperor's.[103] In spring 1524 such fears of French successes were real. From late May, when the French retreated, till October, the French threat in Italy looked less serious. But if the French were to have done spectacularly well in Italy it would have been quite likely that Charles and Francis would have then made peace. If that happened, it would be essential for English honour and security that the terms should be favourable. Throughout the first half of 1524 there was anxiety about French interference in Scotland and the possibility of an invasion across the Scottish borders.[104] For the whole year there was tension between England and France at sea and on land near Calais and Guisnes. Preparations were made in May to send men over to defend Guisnes and Henry said that he would go over in person to defend his ordnance at Valenciennes if that town were besieged.[105] Richard de la Pole was active, as has been seen, in this campaign.[106] It is not surprising that Wolsey wrote to Sampson and Jerningham that Henry trusted that strict regard would be had to his interests if the emperor negotiated peace or a truce with the French.[107] It was such fears that led to the English negotiations with the French in 1524, to which we shall return.

Another important determinant of English policy was the role of Bourbon. If Bourbon continued in rebellion against Francis, if his military campaigns went well, if he offered Henry proper allegiance, then Henry's dreams of conquest might yet be realisable. Much of English diplomacy in 1524 hung on whether Bourbon could be trusted and whether he would be successful. As we have seen, Bourbon had let Henry and Wolsey down in 1523. Wolsey thought he had not acquitted himself as he should and in early 1524 Wolsey struck de Praet as not very affectionately disposed towards him, even though he and the king had just received his emissary.[108] Attitudes towards Bourbon fluctuated considerably in this year. In February Henry invited Bourbon to England for consultations about the proposed expedition.[109] But in late March de Praet wrote that no further money would be given to Bourbon by the English.[110] Policy changed yet again in May: on 7 May Pace was sent to Bourbon, and at the end of May a new alliance had been drawn up.[111]

In the spring of 1524, then, English foreign policy had been fluid. When in March Wolsey had seen 'no certeinte yet knowen here to what purpose, either for werre or peax, the Kinges Grace may trayn his affaires', he was not lying. The king, he said, had not failed, despite imperfect knowledge, 'to stay the maters by good deliberacion avice and counsail, in

suche fourme and maner, that, *howesoever the matiers have succeded,*
. . . it may evidently appere that His Highnes hathe
pretermytted nothing'.[112] Henry and Wolsey were preparing
for all eventualities. They were attracted by a forward policy
that would win honour and strengthen security. But they were
determined not to be let down by the emperor and the
Netherlanders in any new campaign. In turn hopeful and
sceptical of Bourbon's chances, they were anxious to open lines
of contact with the French whenever the French appeared too
successful or whenever Charles and Francis seemed on the
verge of a truce or a peace. In late May 1524 circumstances
favoured a forceful approach. On 25 May a tripartite treaty was
made between Charles, Henry and Bourbon. Bourbon was to
invade France, in Provence, with all speed, supported by king
and emperor; Bourbon was to take an oath of fealty to Henry as
king of France, a condition of receiving English assistance;
Henry was to invade France; Margaret was to assist Henry
with 3,000 horse and 1,000 foot for five months at the emperor's
expense.[113]

Yet English policy remained highly conditional. The king
intended if — and only if — 'by anny great revolution in
Fraunce uppon the duke of Burbons descending there, or by
other victorye, there shalbe commoditie given to his grace to
take anny notable thinges peece or portion . . . then to passe,
eyther in his person, or by his Liewtenaunt, as the case shall
requyre, thoughe yt be in August or September, or latter'. But
the king was 'not mynded to avaunce on this syde, tyll some
great revolution or successe be happened on the other'.[114]
Bourbon was naturally anxious that Henry should support his
own efforts in Provence by invading the north of France as soon
as possible. He was content to swear to Henry as king of France
but unwilling to do him homage, which partial offer Henry
accepted. He appealed to Henry for money. In June he sent one
of his gentlemen to Henry.[115] The problem for Henry and
Wolsey was to assess Bourbon's chances. Pace, Henry's
ambassador with Bourbon, sent home a string of enthusiastic
letters imploring Henry to support Bourbon. Pace saw in
Bourbon 'so faythfull and so stedfast mynde wythowte
vacillation' to help Henry win 'hys crowne of Fraunce, that yff
he be assurydly interteignidde, the Kynge schall assurydly

obteigne hys crown in Fraunce'. 'When we schall lakke the sayde Duke', added Pace, 'we schall nevyr have agayne suche helpe to do any goodde for our selfe in Fraunce'.[116] Now was the time, urged Pace a little later, to take the whole realm of France, or else compel Francis to accept whatever conditions the English laid down. The king was never so likely to recover his rights in France as now.[117] Bourbon wrote that he would not fail in his promise to aid Henry win back his kingdom: on solemn oath he promised to go straight to Reims to see Henry crowned.[118] Pace continued to urge Henry and Wolsey on: by early August Bourbon had conquered more than half France. God, wrote Pace, had taken him under his protection.[119] But Henry and Wolsey remained unconvinced for a long time. They pointed out to Pace that what Bourbon was doing so far was very much in the interests of his private quarrel with Francis; it also furthered Charles' aims; but so far Bourbon had not been particularly successful. If the English sent an army to Picardy it would be very difficult to victual it. Better to wait for a properly organised 'great enterprise' the following year. If, however, Bourbon were to advance to Lyons and then to Paris, that would be more interesting and would encourage Henry to invade.[120] Wolsey wrote even more firmly at the end of August, having just received Sir Gregory de Cassalis as bearer of Pace's letters. He rejoiced to hear of Bourbon's successes. The king and he 'furst aparte' and 'after with the moste sad and discreate lordes of his most honnorable Councell' had discussed the news that Bourbon had taken all of Provence except Marseilles and Arles. Where Pace had gone beyond his commission and urged Henry to invade France, 'yt is consydered here that Provynce is an open and weake countrey, not greatly fortefyed with places of moche strengthe, able to be long kept against an armye' except for Marseilles and Arles, which, Wolsey pointedly noted, were still in French hands. It was very likely that for lack of assistance from the imperialists Bourbon would be compelled to leave Provence. Any English invasion would come too late in the year, and run into difficulties of victualling. So long as Bourbon remained in Provence, and did not advance deeper into France, 'yt were vaine, superfluous, casting away of men and monney, dishonorable, dangerous, and great unwisdome thus late of the yere to avaunce the Kinges sayd armye'. If, however, Bourbon were prepared to give Francis battle, if he were prepared to cross the Rhone, to march towards Lyons and thence aim for 'the bowelles' of France, then Henry was determined to send an army into France in support, possibly led by himself, and to arrange necessary support from the Netherlands.[121] During August and September the consistent thread in English diplomacy was the insistence that if Bourbon marched to Lyons, but only if he did so, then Henry would intervene, provided he could get the help he needed from Margaret.[122] When in late August, just before writing to Pace, Wolsey told de Praet that Henry had decided to order an army to cross at once, or when Henry informed Margaret that he was going to make an invasion, this was still conditional, but shows that preparations were being made in case Bourbon proved victorious.[123] Jerningham was sent to Margaret on 31 August to assist Knight to bargain with her for wagons, limoners, carriages, artillery, ammunition and, above all, the numbers of horse and foot that the Burgundians were to supply.[124] On 10 September a royal circular letter was sent to divers lords and gentlemen to be ready with such power as they could make to assist the king or his lieutenant in an invasion of France.[125] On 2 September Wolsey informed the duke of Norfolk, then on the Scottish borders, that in the light of news from Bourbon via Pace and Cassalis, by whom Henry was strongly urged to seize the opportunity to invade France, which 'by deliberate avice of his counsail [he] is mynded, *the matiers prousperously succeeding*, to do'. He was putting all in readiness: limoners, retaining of landsknechts, negotiations with Margaret. Cassalis was being sent to Bourbon

for perfyte knowlaige to be had of the utter and certain resolucion and actual proceding of that armye on this syde the ryver of Rodan, and other wheyghty and materiall poyntes, *wherupon the avauncing or not avauncing of the Kinges armye on this side shalbe grounded.*[126]

All was still conditional on Bourbon's success: 'every thing put in perfite redines' to be transported at once, wrote Wolsey in late September, 'as sone as knowledge shuld arrive that the said Duke were passed the ryver of Rodan, proceding into the hert and countreys of Fraunce'.[127] But that good news never came. As early as 9 August Russell had written sceptically about

Bourbon's fortunes: apart from Aix he had only won one or two little towns, his rearguard was still in Piedmont, money promised him by the Emperor had not arrived.[128] On 31 August Pace criticised Bourbon's decision (forced upon him by his army) to besiege Marseilles.[129] By late September there were reports of his difficulties; in early October he was compelled to raise the siege and withdraw into Italy.[130] The opportunity for invading France was past. How far had Henry's and Wolsey's doubts been realistic assessments of Bourbon's chances, how far had their refusal to assist because Bourbon was not succeeding become self-fulfilling?

All this time the English had been in contact with the French. What lay behind these negotiations in view of the conditional willingness of Henry to invade France? For Louise of Savoy, the advantages were obvious. Peace with England meant security from the threat of English invasion, freedom from the distraction of a northern campaign while Francis was fighting in the south. For Henry and Wolsey negotiations with the French were above all an insurance in case the French were devastatingly successful in Italy or in case Charles and Francis, prompted as they were by the pope in spring 1524 and no doubt could be again at any time, made a private peace without consulting the English. In May de Praet noted Wolsey's fear that peace might be concluded without much regard for English interests.[131] Moreover negotiations might, after all, produce an honourable peace. The campaigns of 1522 and 1523 had shown how limited was the assistance Henry could expect from Charles and Margaret; those of 1523 and 1524 had shown Bourbon up as a weak reed. Perhaps it was in Henry's best interests to look for a deal with the French. On the other hand, while such negotiations would undoubtedly annoy the imperialists, they might nonetheless encourage them to offer Henry better terms and greater assistance should changing circumstances produce another opportunity for a joint attack on France.

It was in April 1524, when the French were doing well in Italy, and expectations of a papal 'peace initiative' were high, that Jean Joachim de Passano, seigneur de Vaux, Louise of Savoy's maître d'hôtel came to England.[132] Wolsey dealt with Joachim himself and did not stint his demands: Normandy,

Guyenne and Gascony, and the crown of France were sought for Henry. Or so Wolsey told de Praet.[133] With French reverses in May, negotiations seem to have petered out and Joachim was apparently sent away, to return in early June.[134] There is little evidence that detailed bargaining took place at first. Joachim was treated cordially in August, just as Henry and Wolsey were apparently about to send an army across to France if Bourbon did well: was that intended to bid up terms from the imperialists?[135] While English intentions to invade were, as has been argued above, serious, if conditional, they did of course have the advantage of increasing pressure on the French in negotiations, though there is little sign of any progress in August or September. After Bourbon's campaign had failed and once Francis' counter-attack in Italy became known in October, news that brought fears of important French successes, negotiations with Joachim appear to take on a more important tone and details (presumably far from trustworthy) of them play an increasingly prominent part in de Praet's letters.[136] Yet if de Praet is right that the English continued to demand lands from Francis, it is likely that he was also right to report that the negotiations were on the verge of failure in November.[137]

Another aspect of Anglo-French bargaining was of course Scotland. Henry and Wolsey were always alert to the threat that Scotland could become a satellite of France and a springboard for an invasion. That seemed the more likely during the minority of the young king James V given the prominent role of John Stewart, duke of Albany. Albany's father was James III's brother and hence James IV's uncle: his mother was a French noblewoman, and he had been born and brought up in France. After James IV's death at Flodden, Albany had been invited to govern Scotland during James V's minority and he had been resident regent from May 1515 to June 1517. His departure was part of Francis I's overtures of peace towards the English and until late 1521 Francis restrained Albany's ambitions. But once it became clear to the French king that Henry VIII was making a new alliance with Charles V, Francis supplied Albany with ships and soldiers and sent him to make trouble for Henry. Albany returned to

Scotland in late 1521: in September 1522 Henry had to raise a large army to defend the northern borders against a feared Scottish invasion sponsored by the French and led by Albany. Even though Albany failed to stir the Scottish nobility to make the greatest efforts and left Scotland in October, in early 1523 Henry and Wolsey were still sufficiently concerned by the threat he posed to put dealing with the Scots ahead of joining with the emperor against the French until persuaded otherwise by the rebellion of Bourbon.[138] In September 1523 Albany returned to Scotland and cajoled the Scots to assist him in a siege of the English border fortress of Wark. In the event that siege failed ignominiously and the threatened subsequent invasion of England did not take place.[139] But if there were now few immediate worries here for Henry, nonetheless the situation might look very different should a triumphant Francis return from Italy and encourage Albany to try his luck once more, especially if Richard de la Pole were to be involved as well. Even if negotiations with the French were not very seriously intended, they could nonetheless, if they deterred the French from interfering, help to maintain peace on the northern borders. That, Wolsey told de Praet in July 1524, was their purpose.[140]

In late 1523 an intricate series of negotiations began between Queen Margaret and Albany on the Scottish side, Wolsey and Lord Dacre, warden of the west marches, on the English side. In response to some Scottish raiding in February 1524, attempts were made by the English to raise men in February and March, and Wolsey urged further raids to annoy the Scots and to put further pressure on Albany: but finally Albany left for France in June 1524.[141] Anglo-French negotiations might help to prevent his return. More substantial dealing then took place between queen Margaret and the duke of Norfolk, sent up to the Scottish borders in summer 1524. The English wanted to see peace on the borders, the declaration of the majority and the coronation of the young king (which would imply a restriction of Albany's influence) and the end of French interference in Scotland. Negotiations continued throughout the summer and autumn of 1524: eventually Scottish ambassadors came to London in December.[142] Scottish threats to England could, then, be discounted: English hopes of diplomatic success were high, a good reason for not provoking the French into upsetting them.

At the beginning of 1525 the direction of English foreign policy remained, as it had been, pro-imperial, because the ruler of the Netherlands was England's natural ally just as the French were the traditional enemy, and because, on the whole, in the Habsburg-Valois struggle, the Habsburgs seemed to be the stronger; yet there was a reluctance to commit forces and money to an invasion of France without substantial support from the Netherlands, an evident fear of serving as a catspaw for the imperialists (resulting from vivid memories of how the English had been let down in recent campaigns); there were also negotiations of varying seriousness with the French to insure against a separate Franco-imperial peace, against the possibility, which occasionally seemed high, of imperial losses in Italy, and against the chance of French mischief-making on the Scottish borders. This called for a delicate balancing act as news from Italy and perceptions of Francis' and Charles' intentions changed.

What is remarkable is that just as the English had become very cautious about the prospects for a successful campaign in France, so the imperialists were urging, with increasing stridency, that Henry should take immediate action. This reflected their growing difficulties in Italy, which in themselves could only reinforce Henry's and Wolsey's caution lest they allied themselves too closely with the losing side. In mid-December 1524 Charles appealed to them to take the field in person or at least to send an army across. De Praet was ordered to point out to the king and minister the opportunity of conquering France.[143] De Praet frequently pressed Wolsey in January 1525 but in vain: nothing could be done till the end of April.[144] All they would do was to send some money via Russell to assist Charles' Italian campaign.[145] Charles implored Wolsey that now was the time to act and sent over a special envoy, Cilly.[146] Margaret despatched three commissioners, Bèvres, Laurens and de la Sauch in late January, with special powers to make concessions on the number of horse and foot and the price of victual that the Netherlanders would supply in support of an English campaign. In early March they saw Wolsey but he and the king told them it was too early in the year and laid down tough conditions.[147] On several occasions Wolsey complained of earlier failings by the imperialists. Henry had spent enormous sums and conquered nothing. Charles had in numerous ways infringed treaties he had made with Henry. The imperialists had not handled matters well in Italy.[148] Henry and Wolsey had become very cautious about the chances of imperial support for their efforts, but it is worth noting that in these months they were under unusually intense pressure from Charles to assist his cause, and that pressure, rather than any intention to throw off the alliance, explains the strength of their expressions of unwillingness to embark on a military campaign at an unfavourable time of year.

Anglo-imperial relations were further complicated, and envenomed, by Wolsey's quarrel with de Praet, Charles' ambassador. In the night of 11 February, some of de Praet's letters were intercepted, opened, read and found to be critical of Wolsey. Was the seizure of the letters deliberate? Was it intended to serve as an excuse — a justification — for a rupture with the imperialists, as has been suggested? Or was it all chance, appalling bad luck as it turned out? Wolsey gave an official account of the incident in his letter to Sampson on 13 February. A man carrying a little packet of letters, superscribed in French, suspected of being a spy, was taken during a watch and brought to More and then to Wolsey. Wolsey read the letters and found them 'ferre . . . discrepant from the trouthe'. He accused de Praet of having 'don more hurte detryment and dammage by his evil reaportes in the common affaires, then ever he can be able to redubbe or amende'. As a result de Praet was effectively expelled.[149] Obviously this could be seen as deliberate provocation by the English to disrupt Anglo-imperial relations, as proof that Wolsey had 'la volonté arrêtée de rompre avec Praet'.[150] But there is no reason to explain why Henry or Wolsey should have wished at this moment to make any such break. News from the battlefield was inconclusive. Negotiations with the French were continuing but, to say the least, far from settled. Nor is it clear why Henry and Wolsey would have wished so blatantly to declare their change of alliance if that is what they were doing. It is far more likely that Wolsey was quite sincerely annoyed. He had been critical of de Praet for some time. In March 1524 he had told Sampson and Jerningham that 'by suche conjectures as may be had here', de Praet 'being a man not of most experience and conduyte in suche affaires' made 'many tymes synistre reaport', judging from Charles' reactions.[151] 'It hath ben of a longe season and from sundry parties reaported unto the Kinges Highnes and to me at diverse tymes', wrote Wolsey in February 1525, that de Praet 'hathe contynually ben a man disposed and inclyned to make in his letters and writinges . . . sedicious and sinistre reaportes, faynyng many tymes, upon his oune fantasie suspicion or conjecture, thinges clerely untrue.'[152] De Praet had undoubtedly written critically in autumn 1524. In November Wolsey accused him of telling lies about Wolsey and the king and threatened to demand his recall. De Praet noted in December that for some time he had felt that Wolsey did not trust him.[153] Wolsey could quite reasonably have been annoyed by what de Praet wrote in the seized letters. 'Si nous pourrions gaigner la batail', de Praet had suggested, referring to Italy, 'tout ira bien lors que nostre maistre se boute hors de dangier de telz amys et confederez . . . . Et fault encores que je dye quil est peu tenu a eulx tous, tant quilz sont . . . . Jespere de voir une foix nostre maistre vengie', against, it seems he meant, Wolsey.[154] Comments of this kind must have reinforced Henry's and Wolsey's worst fears of Charles' intentions and further reduced their hopes of obtaining any support from him for an eventual invasion of France. But it remains likely that it was just chance that de Praet's letters were intercepted.

Moreover to suggest that Henry or Wolsey were looking for ways to break their alliance with the imperialists is to claim that Anglo-French relations were more friendly than they were. Joachim had indeed spent a long time in England. But was this 'une preuve assurée que le Cardinal estimait les propositions de Madame capables de servir de bases à un accord entre les deux gouvernements'[155] or was it rather a continuing insurance, as has been suggested above, against French victories in Italy, a separate Franco-imperial peace and French interference in Scotland? Just how warm were Anglo-French negotiations in early 1525? However suspicious he was of Joachim, de Praet never gave up trying to persuade Wolsey and Henry to join with the emperor and invade France. The arrival in England of

Brinon, president of the parlement of Normandy at Rouen, in late January[156] might suggest that negotiations were becoming more serious, but there is very little evidence for this. Louise of Savoy's instructions of 16 February, acknowledging a letter sent by Brinon and Joachim on 29 January, make it clear that Wolsey had been driving a very hard bargain and had not got very far. He had been seeking, among other demands, Boulogne, Guisnes and Ardres. Louise ordered her agents to tell Wolsey that Francis would never agree to yield an inch of his territory.[157] Brinon's and Joachim's letter of 6 March strengthens the argument that negotiations had been hard and unsuccessful. Wolsey had told them that if they made no more concessions he would bid them adieu, that he was expecting ambassadors from Flanders and that then he would put everything in readiness for war and send money to those fighting against the French in Italy. Their answer, Wolsey insisted, omitted the principal point, Henry's claim to lands in France, without which no peace could be made. Wolsey had gone on to demand the payment of principal and arrears owing for Tournai. If, as this letter suggests, Henry and Wolsey were going to insist on obtaining lands from the French before making peace, then peace was some way off. And if all this was negotiators' bluff, it still suggests that no deal was yet in the making by early March.[158] True, Brinon and Joachim were due to see Henry on 9 March, but the expectations of peace reported by Hall based on this imminent visit seem premature.[159] Henry and Wolsey were doing no more than keeping their options open: in early 1525 they were certainly not committed, nor on the point of making a commitment, to a French alliance.

The most illuminating evidence for English policy at that time is a letter that Wolsey sent to the king on 12 February (just after the seizure of de Praet's letters). Wolsey summed up military and diplomatic news from Italy. Henry, he then continued, was in an excellent position. If the imperialists won, 'the thanke, laude and praise shal comme unto Your Grace', because of the money Henry had recently sent to assist them; but if 'perceace, by any adverse chaunce, thEmperiallis shulde be inferiours, wherin ther is non apparance' — indeed Wolsey went on to conclude his letter 'abidyng knowlege of the further successes [of the imperialists], which cannot faile to be had shortely' — 'yet, thanked be God, your affaires be, by your highe wisedome, in more assured and substancial trayne, by such communications as be set furth with France apart, then others in outewarde places wolde suppose'.[160] This is the key to English diplomacy before Pavia. Henry and Wolsey were expecting, and hoping for, an imperial victory in Italy which they trusted would enable them to launch a joint Anglo-imperial campaign in France; and yet they wished to insure themselves against the chance, however slight, of French success in the battlefield. Because of the disappointments and mistrust of 1522–3 they were unwilling to risk a more forward policy (which the imperialists were urging on them) in autumn 1524 or winter 1524–5, as this could have led to further disasters. It would also, of course, have destroyed the insurance offered by negotiations with the French. Where Wolsey's analysis was seriously flawed, however, was in its assumption that despite English unwillingness to invade France, thus creating the diversion of French pressure on him that Charles needed so badly while the campaigns in Italy were proving inconclusive, the imperialists would nonetheless be grateful for the very limited financial aid that Henry and Wolsey were sending south. De Praet expressed imperial annoyance, and the dangers of English policy, on 7 March in language similar to that in his letters intercepted a month earlier:

if we can only gain this battle [in Italy], all will go well with the Emperor, our master, provided he can afterward disengage himself from the ties of his friends and confederates, to whom, I do not hesitate to say, he owes but little gratitude.[161]

In early January 1525 Charles had jotted down his private thoughts: 'the king of England does not help me as a true friend should; he does not even help me to the extent of his obligations'.[162]

The astonishingly overwhelming imperial victory at Pavia on 24 February in which the king of France was not only defeated but humiliatingly captured revived ambitions but also created problems for the English. Suddenly the ancient enemy lay prone and seemingly defenceless. It appeared an ideal moment to assert legitimate English claims. Ironically it would be the English who would press for an invasion of France while the imperialists, who had been urging on Henry and Wolsey for months, would now see little need for further military action, especially in support of an ally who had been, in their eyes, less than ready to assist just before. Henry was delighted by the news of Pavia which arrived on 9 March. The imperial commissioners found him in very high spirits, beaming with joy. 'Now is the time', he said, 'for the emperor and myself to devise the means of getting full satisfaction from France: not an hour is to be lost'.[163] Another account, whose source is uncertain, tells how Henry was unable to read the news 'without crying with joy', praising God, and comparing the messenger to Angel Gabriel announcing the arrival of Christ.[164] Bonfires were organised in the city of London; on Sunday, Wolsey, assisted by four bishops and six abbots, celebrated the great victory by officiating himself at a *Te Deum*, with great numbers of noblemen present, at St Paul's Cathedral.[165] The council met on 10 March and determined on war against France.[166]

What were Henry's ambitions after Pavia? Bishop Tunstall and Sir Richard Wingfield, the trusted servants whom Henry was sending to Charles in Spain, were ordered to assert Henry's demands. He claimed 'by just title of enheritance to have the hole crown of Fraunce, as that whiche oweth to descende unto hym of veray right and succession'; and even without that, the duchies of Normandy, Gascony, Guyenne, Anjou, Maine, Poitou and other patrimonies unjustly detained by the French king which of right belonged to Henry 'by lyke lyniall discent and succession'. Henry suggested that Charles and he meet at Paris, where Henry would be crowned king of France, and then Henry would accompany Charles to Rome to see the crown imperial placed on his head. 'Oon of the chife and prinicipal thinges intended and convented' by Henry and Charles 'hath alwaies ben to expell the Frenche king from his usurped occupacion of the croune of Fraunce, and to conduce the Kinges Highnes, as right requireth, unto the same'. France might then be divided three ways between Henry, the emperor and the duke of Bourbon. Charles would get Provence, Languedoc as far as Toulouse, and the duchy of Burgundy; Bourbon would get his patrimony and Dauphiné; Henry would get the rest. If Charles was unwilling to deprive Francis of his crown, then Henry demanded Normandy, Gascony, Guyenne, Anjou, Maine, Poitou, Brittany and Picardy: at least Picardy, Normandy and Thérouanne, or at the very least Normandy with a pension.[167] In mid-to-late April Sir William Fitzwilliam and Sir Robert Wingfield, sent to Margaret in the Netherlands, were instructed to assert that Henry had a right to the whole crown of France, by inheritance and by treaties; and even if that were denied, Henry claimed Normandy, Gascony, Guyenne, Anjou, Maine and Poitou.[168] Such claims were nothing new. In April 1524, for example, Henry had told the papal legate of 'many recordes, prouyng the kyng of England to be inheritor to the realme of Fraunce by bloud and also so confirmed by diuers charters in the tyme of kyng Charles the vii'; the pension that Henry had intermittently received from the French was as rent for the duchies of Normandy, Guyenne, Anjou and Maine 'which are the kyng of Englandes very inheritaunce'.[169] In 1525 such ambitions were asserted in support of Henry's financial demands. In late March or early April Wolsey spoke to Londoners. He gave an historical account of efforts that had failed to make and to preserve peace between England and France, of how despite covenants made and sworn, despite the meeting of Henry and Francis at the king's 'greate cost and charge', Francis had refused to keep the peace with Charles in 1520–1 and had spurned Wolsey's mediation in 1521. He appealed to the Londoners to consider how the French seized and imprisoned English merchants at Bordeaux 'whiche the Turke would not haue doen'. 'Whiche thynges you knowe', summed up Wolsey, 'the kyng of his honor might not suffre'. Twice, as a result, France had been invaded (1522, 1523). The English had 'burnt their townes, castles and fortresses, destroyed the people . . . and . . . brought the countrey in such penury and wretchednes, that in many yeres it will not be recouered'. Because Henry had kept Bourbon in wages, and sent 100,000 crowns to Italy, Francis had been defeated and taken prisoner 'to the Emperor and the kyng our Master', an interpretation that exaggerated Henry's role. Since God had given victory, Henry remembering that, as the poet had said, it was more mastery to use victory gotten, than to get it, thought it necessary 'now in all hast' to make an army royal and to lead it in person across the seas, 'to recouer his right inheritaunce, bothe of the croune of Fraunce as of Normandie, Guyen, Gascone, Aniowe and Mayne'.[170] The preamble of the instructions sent to Archbishop Warham for the grant from the spirituality of his diocese justified royal intentions. It began by describing events up to Pavia. Peace had been 'violated and broken' by the French king, 'auncient enemye' to this realm. Bourbon had on oath recognised Henry as king of France. Pavia now gave the opportunity of regaining the crown and territories of France 'rightfully apperteynyng vnto the kinges highnes'.[171] Henry's letter to the mayor, aldermen and citizens of London of 25 April spoke of his 'intended voyage into Fraunce for recouery and atteignynge of our crowne and rightes there'.[172] What Henry sought was the crown of France and, or at least, several provinces formerly held by kings of England. Of course there was a good deal of rhetoric in this propaganda. Although such claims were not new, they had not been put forward consistently in a sustained campaign of persuasion, and the suddenness and boldness with which they were now asserted made them far from convincing. Some of the propaganda was very offhand. Speaking to Londoners, Wolsey referred to the king's claims to various French provinces, 'the writynges whereof comprehendyng the very title, you maie se here present if ye list, but I doubt not but you knowe them well inough'.[173] These claims did not arouse any crescendo of popular anti-French feeling. But nonetheless they did represent Henry's hopes immediately after Pavia and if the imperialists had good reasons for criticising the English for their lack of recent assistance, Charles did all the same present English demands for the cession of Normandy, Guyenne and Gascony as his own in April.[174] The problem for Henry would be how to enforce his rights.

What military strategy did Henry and Wolsey intend to pursue to secure these ambitions? On 10 March Wolsey told the imperial commissioners that Henry intended to invade France, landing on the coast of Normandy at the end of May: the duke of Norfolk would cross over first and make for Valenciennes, where royal ordnance was stored.[175] On 16 March Wolsey repeated that Henry intended to invade Normandy in person.[176] Picardy, he later insisted, after briefly appearing to toy with the possibility of an invasion there, was too strongly fortified. Since Henry intended to lead the army in person, he had to attack some region less strongly defended. A large army of 20,000 foot and 2,000 horse under Norfolk and 20,000 foot under the king could not be victualled in Picardy. The English would go from Calais to Montreuil-sur-mer, Thérouanne, Hesdin, then via Beauce into Normandy. Henry certainly wished to invade France in person and clearly preferred to aim at Normandy.[177] But early in April Wolsey convinced him that in view of the difficulty of this plan, the lack of firm knowledge of Charles' intentions and the uncertainty of the raising of revenue, he should wait:

remembring . . . that passing into Normandy the Kinges Highnes can not furnishe hym self of no les vitailes than for viii daies, whiche wolbe veray difficile to do. And that vitaile spent or not spent it is doubtefull howe the passage may be had by Blanchetake [Blanche Tâche ford] whiche failing the kinges grace shuld haue on his bake Monstrel, Heding, Tirwin and Boleyn.

Wolsey went on that he had

for thise causes by great persuasions induced the kinges highnes to be contented that my lord of Norfolke with his vauntgarde And those appointed in the reregarde whiche in the hole woll amount vnto the nombre of [xx]ml men or more besides the aide of Flaunders shall somwhat in the more diligence passe bifore. And that his grace shal demore here till such tyme as more certayntye may be had as wel of themperors mynde and intente Howe the money may be levyed And also what shal succede of taking the said passage of Blanchetak.[178]

Norfolk was duly appointed lieutenant of the vanguard on 11 April. He was to land at Calais and then capture Blanchetake. A book was prepared listing those noblemen, together with their retinues, who were to accompany him. Wolsey expected the army to number 20,000. Sir William Fitzwilliam would be marshall, Sir Thomas Cheney assistant. The posts of master of ordnance, treasurers of ordnance, comptroller, provost and other offices were filled. Lord Fitzwalter and Sir Robert Wingfield would form Norfolk's council. Victuallers were to be appointed that day. On 13 April letters would be sent to all those going in person or sending men.[179] Norfolk delightedly acknowledged his appointment.[180] On 12 April Sir William Fitzwilliam and Sir Robert Wingfield were sent to Margaret to prepare the campaign.[181] Their instructions included details of provisions, carriages, limoners and shipping that were to be supplied by Margaret. They made specific practical arrangements. They would pay out £3,061 8s. 8d. in advance payments for 1,460 limoners and 1,230 wagons. They persuaded Margaret to agree to the appointment of a number of hoys at the emperor's expense but they had to argue strongly to win her assent.[182] Men were being recruited in the north of England from where Sir William Bulmer, Sir William Eure, Sir Thomas Tempest, John Bentley and W. Franklin reported their progress on 27 April.[183] The duke of Norfolk was returning to East Anglia in late April in order to raise men.[184] How successful would an English invasion of France have been in 1525? The Scots expected that Henry would gain Paris. The bishop of Bayeux thought that the best way of preserving the kingdom of France was to make a deal with Henry: he greatly feared English might.[185] But there is little sign of serious military preparations in April or May. When Wolsey told the imperial commissioners in early May that corn, barley, oats, salt meat and other provisions had already been stored on board the royal fleet, and that these would be spoilt if they were not soon used, he was most probably bluffing.[186] None of the Public Record Office series which yield much information about the organisation of campaigns of 1522 and 1523 show that any planning of supplies was taking place at all. A year later Francis I told an English negotiator that though if Henry had made war in earnest 'I should have fellt yt much grevouslyer' than before, nevertheless 'I know right well yt was but ceremonyously done'.[187] In retrospect there does appear an element of 'make believe' about the campaign. Clearly Henry and Wolsey, despite their grand ambitions, and forward military strategy, were biding their time, waiting to see just what support they would get from Charles and the Netherlands and to see how well the Amicable Grant would be paid.

Henry and Wolsey made surprisingly little effort to contact Bourbon. On 11 March Russell wrote that Bourbon was willing to set the French crown on Henry's head.[188] On 25 April Russell wrote that Bourbon's army would need substantial support from Henry.[189] On 16 May Russell wrote that Bourbon thought it long since he heard from England and was sorry to

see so fair a time wasted.[190] On 26 May Russell repeated that
Bourbon was surprised not to have heard from Henry and
Wolsey.[191] Not till 18 May did Wolsey write.[192] Were king and
minister thoroughly disillusioned by Bourbon's efforts in 1523
and 1524? Did they now feel that the support they needed could
only come from the imperialists?

Bargaining with the Netherlanders began on 10 March, the
same day that the council resolved on war with France. Henry
wanted 3,000 horse and 1,000 foot from the Netherlanders.[193]
On 16 March Wolsey increased these demands to 3,000–4,000
horse and 3,000 foot.[194] Margaret and her advisers reacted
stiffly to these proposals, in particular rejecting the idea of
assisting the English with horse and foot in Normandy.[195]
Negotiations continued in difficulties in early April.
Discussions turned on whether the English should attack in
Normandy or Picardy and how these forces would be
victualled.[196] In late April these negotiations ended
inconclusively with Margaret's commissioners declaring that
they had no authority to make any agreement, even if Henry
and Wolsey agreed to their terms.[197] Mutual mistrust was high.
The Netherlanders made Henry's scheme of invading
Normandy public and thereby lessened its attractions;[198] the
English threatened to break off their alliance and join with
the pope, the Venetians, Florentines and French and drive the
imperialists out of Italy.[199] Sir William Fitzwilliam and Sir
Robert Wingfield were sent from Guisnes and Calais, two
experienced and trusted negotiators, to see Margaret and
bargain with her for appropriate assistance, which, as we have
seen, they did in detail. On 2 May they reached agreement that
Margaret would supply 3,000 horse and 1,000 foot at the
emperor's expense.[200]

But the crucial attitude was that of Charles in Spain. Henry
and Wolsey thought it essential that he support English action.
They immediately sent him letters congratulating him on Pavia
and announcing the imminent despatch of an honourable
personage to discuss what they should do next, letters which
arrived on 25 March.[201] But some time then elapsed before
ambassadors were appointed. Possibly it was thought at first
that Wolsey should go. However that may be, the commissions
naming and letters instructing Sir Richard Wingfield and

Bishop Tunstall were all dated 26 March.[202] Wingfield and
Tunstall were to join Sampson, who was already with Charles,
and to negotiate for a joint personal invasion of France by
Charles and Henry later that year. Long and elaborate orders
were issued.[203] The embassy was a disaster. Tunstall and
Wingfield were at Southampton on 7 and 10 April waiting for
ships at Portsmouth to be made ready, still at Southampton on
14 April, and on 19 April forced by storms to land at Hamble.
Tempests, vividly described in a letter of 30 April, then spoiled
their voyage to Spain, compelling them to land at Ribadir,
fifteen days from Toledo. Not till 24 May, two months after
their impending arrival was notified to Charles, did they reach
Toledo.[204] By then, of course, the Amicable Grant had failed
and English intentions were rather different. It was highly
sensible to send ambassadors to Charles but unfortunate that
their journey took so long.

Sampson, meanwhile, was writing discouragingly about the
attitudes of Charles. He was quite right: in late March Charles
noted that it sounded badly to make war upon a prisoner
unable to defend himself.[205] Sampson wrote how Charles
intended to use his victory to establish universal peace in
Christendom and how Charles felt less bound to Henry because
of Joachim's long residence in England and because of the
quarrel over de Praet. He was disposed to peace; he wished
Henry to have an army ready but not to use it if good means of
peace might be found.[206] By 1 April Sampson had become
convinced that there was no hope of the aid of 3,000 horse and
3,000 foot at the emperor's expense that Henry was seeking.
Some of the emperor's council had made it plain to him that
Henry should not do marvels against a prisoner.[207] Sampson's
next letter, written on 2 May, was even more discouraging.
Charles' chancellor had thought it 'not well possible' to
attempt a joint personal invasion of France that year: the
emperor had sustained too great charges.[208] But it is likely that
Henry and Wolsey did not see these letters with their
pessimistic implications for Henry's ambitions until after the
Amicable Grant had failed. On 14 April Tunstall wondered
why Sampson's letters had not arrived: presumably nothing
had come from him by then that had been written after news of
Pavia had reached Spain.[209] It was not until the end of May

that Wolsey received Sampson's letter of (presumably) 2 May. By 27 May, on receiving Sampson's letter, Wolsey had come to see the campaign as hopeless. 'Your Grace', he wrote to the king, 'shall receyve the same herwith, and right sone shal understand therby, that such werre, as the said Emperour intendith to provoke your Highnes unto, shal lytel or nothing be to your commodite, proufit, or benefit', this because it was clear that Charles would give no worthwhile assistance.[210]

From the moment that news of Pavia had arrived, English hopes of pursuing claims in France had depended not only on obtaining money but also on securing assistance from the emperor. Perhaps Henry's and Wolsey's hopes were never that great. Those instructions to Tunstall and Wingfield with their grandiose schemes for the dismemberment of France were arranged as a series of proposals in descending order: Henry's and Wolsey's minimum was set fairly low.[211] No very detailed military preparations were made, as we have seen. Threats to leave the alliance were made against the Netherlanders in April. But little thought was given to the possibility of Henry acting on his own. In October 1524 Sampson, sceptical of imperial assistance, advised Henry that if he wanted to advance his interests he should trust only to his own army and strength, and if by chance he received support from others, he should treat it as a bonus, for generally it was every man for himself.[212] One of Wolsey's remarks to Tunstall and Wingfield in early April was 'howe his highnes regarding only his own commodite might right well do his feate withoute themperor';[213] Wolsey also suggested to the imperial commissioners that Henry might act alone and nonetheless be crowned king of France.[214] But there is nothing to suggest that Henry or Wolsey ever saw independent action as a serious military possibility. It is worth asking whether they were right, whether a quick thrust might have achieved a *fait accompli* that Charles and the Netherlanders would have seen as in their interest eventually to support. By late May it was clear to Wolsey that the assistance that he thought essential would not be forthcoming from the emperor. This reinforced the failure of the Amicable Grant in ending hopes of a campaign against the French in 1525. There is a marked difference in tone in Wolsey's negotiations with the imperial ambassadors. In early

May Wolsey was urging them that the time had come to attack the common enemy, that if the summer was allowed to pass it would be too late. By mid-to-late May Wolsey was less friendly. There were no discussions of military matters and Henry and Wolsey were unhelpful over safeconducts. The imperial commissioners were preparing to leave. By 13 June one of them could confidently report that there was no great probability of war being made by the English that season.[215] In mid-to-late May, as a result of the failure of the Amicable Grant and the increasingly obvious lack of assistance from the imperialists, Henry and Wolsey abandoned any intentions of fighting the French. Joachim, who had left England in March, was back by late June[216] and negotiations with the French that were to produce the treaty of the More began in earnest as Henry and Wolsey sought not to be left out if Charles and Francis made peace.

This analysis of English foreign policy in the years leading up to the Amicable Grant has assumed that Henry and Wolsey were working together and in broad agreement. There is nothing to show that Wolsey was acting independently of Henry, that the king was no more than a mouthpiece for the cardinal. In the last resort, Wolsey was always Henry's servant, and the policy he executed was his master's. Of course Wolsey did far more of the work of discussing diplomatic, legal and military details with ambassadors than did the king but that is neither surprising nor evidence of any lack of royal interest.[217] Stray remarks, taken out of context, might suggest that Henry was lazy or inefficient, but careful reading quickly disposes of such an interpretation. For example, on 10 November 1524 de Praet wrote that Henry had never taken less interest in affairs than he did then, and it was therefore very important that Wolsey should receive his pension from the emperor, as he did everything here. Yet earlier in the same letter de Praet described how he had been with Henry in early November. Henry had spoken bitterly and in detail about Bourbon's campaign, blamed the imperialists for not giving support and then drew de Praet aside to ask two favours from Charles concerning the bishopric of Malta and the duke of Milan. Moreover in a slightly later letter de Praet wrote how when he

asked Wolsey that the English should contribute to the defence
of Milan, Wolsey went to discuss it with Henry before giving a
decision. This is not a description of an idle monarch neglecting
public affairs.[218] Because ambassadors mainly saw Wolsey
they perhaps attributed too much significance to him and too
little to the king and to other counsellors (whose role, as
revealed by their letters, is shadowy). Wolsey was aware of
de Praet's view of him, and angrily rejected it,

saying . . . that His Grace is a Prince of suche grete wisedome knowlege and
experience in his affaires, that I, whome His Highnes dothe put in so singuler
trust and special confidence, wolde be lothe to say or do anything in so grete
maters as thise be, bifore I had first well and substancially knowen the mynde
and pleasure of his Grace, and ben by the same commaunded so to do: ne I
may or wol of my self take vppon me, withoute the auctorite knowlege and
expresse commaundement of His Highnes, either to do or undo . . . but
rather it shuld seme that the said Ambassadour wolde think or meane that
either my master is a Prince of smal knowlaige or counsail, that I may do in
his grete affaires what I woll

or would impute to the king the criticisms he was making of
Wolsey.[219] It was always a temptation, as Peter Gwyn has
shown, for an ambassador displeased at the state of events to
blame the leading minister for everything: if only Wolsey was
not so influential, all would be well.[220] But this could be self-
delusion. When in September 1524 de Praet complained that
Henry was always changeable and attributed this to the fact
that he always agreed with Wolsey and whatever Wolsey
wished him to do, he was surely mistaken. The changeability of
attitudes in that month was, as we have seen, simply part of a
general policy of waiting upon events, of making preparations
for an invasion of France while insisting that the final decision
would depend on reports of how well Bourbon was doing.
De Praet misread fluid policy as the result (somewhat
contradictorily) of a fickle king influenced by a fickle minister.
When de Praet went on to say that Wolsey was trying to shift
the blame for any possible failure on to Charles, so as to excuse
himself to the king, he was, despite his earlier remarks,
implying Henry's dominance.[221] It was Henry's practice to
react to reports and diplomatic proposals only when these were
important. In October 1523 the earl of Surrey wrote that he was
sorry that Henry and Wolsey were so far apart: this delayed

answers to his letters. Wolsey marvelled at Surrey's complaint
that he was not speedily answered: 'the king is not accustomed
so often times, to make answer to letters containing only news,
wherein, peraventure, amongst twenty there is scarcely two
found true'. Significantly Henry did write to Surrey a little later
about the Scottish assault against Wark castle and Albany's
flight in November.[222] Henry was indeed not always physically
close to Wolsey but he always took a close interest in important
events. During the campaign of autumn 1523 letters were sent
between Wolsey and Henry (Henry's being written by Sir
Thomas More, the king's secretary). Henry's absence from
London was not because he could not care less about what was
happening. On the contrary, he was often eager to know the
latest news. In November 1524, when Henry was again apart
from Wolsey, Henry interrupted More who was about to say
what letters he brought, by guessing, wrongly as it turned out,
that More was bringing letters from Joachim, Louise of Savoy's
agent in England. Then Henry 'fell meryly to the redyng of the
lettres of maister Pace, and all the other abstractes and
wrytinges'.[223] Letters were most often written to Wolsey, but
sometimes to both Wolsey and the king, and important letters
were addressed to the king. Wolsey forwarded letters addressed
to himself.[224] Henry was always kept informed. He knew, as
More's letter just quoted shows, of Joachim's presence in
England and about Wolsey's negotiations with him. In
February 1525 Wolsey was delighted and relieved to learn from
More how the king had been pleased with his discussions with
Brinon, sent by Louise of Savoy to join Joachim, for a peace
treaty.[225] Possibly Hall was right that Joachim 'never was seen
with the kyng',[226] though it is quite likely that Henry may have
met him at Hampton Court in August 1524;[227] what is
abundantly clear is that Wolsey's dealings with the French
were in no way a private initiative — Henry knew, was kept
informed, and approved, of what was done. Moreover Henry
did see ambassadors himself. In June 1523 Henry saw the
imperial ambassadors, drawing one of them apart; Henry was
with Wolsey when de Praet gave them news from Charles in
late July; Beaurain's secretary was heard first by Wolsey and
then by Henry in August; de Praet had an audience with the
king in late August; Bourbon's gentleman was affably

received by Henry in October; d'Aerschot and de Praet saw the king in late October or early November; Lurey, another gentleman sent by Bourbon, saw both Wolsey and Henry in November; and so on.[228] Nor was Henry in any sense a dummy wheeled on stage by an all-powerful minister for ceremonial effect. Henry's audiences were serious. In May 1523 de Praet thought it worthwhile to set down Henry's replies to his demands word for word.[229] In June 1525 the imperial ambassadors had two conferences with Henry and Wolsey of six to seven hours each and another with Wolsey alone of four hours.[230] Henry had strong views of his own. After complaining to de Praet about the failure of the emperor to pay previously agreed indemnities, Henry went on to complain again so much to his household that Queen Catherine sent her confessor to de Praet to warn him of the depth of Henry's discontent.[231] De Praet thought it worthwhile to have several friends among the king's intimates, not to influence him, but to report his attitudes to an invasion of France, evidence of their importance.[232] Crucial decisions, especially in response to a military event, or a new offer or a firm refusal in diplomatic bargaining, were not made by Wolsey alone. In 1523 Lord Sandys, sent by Suffolk from the frontline in France, went to Henry at Windsor and declared his message; Henry then went to Wolsey's house at Westminster, received further letters from Suffolk and sent news to Suffolk of Mountjoy's preparations.[233] In April 1525, as we have seen, Henry was set on beginning his invasion of France in Normandy. Once the imperial commissioners had convinced Wolsey, after a series of discussions, that it was quite impossible for them to assist in such a strategy, Wolsey eventually said that he would have to see Henry and tell him of the difficulties. This he did; Henry then saw the commissioners himself and attempted to reach a compromise.[234] Henry and Wolsey obviously discussed diplomacy and military plans: they made a good team, differing on occasions on particular targets, as in September 1523, but united throughout this period on a fundamental article of policy, namely that any English invasion of France required support from the emperor, the Netherlands and Bourbon, and so was always conditional.

This makes it hard to see king and cardinal as fundamentally opposed, to see Henry as warlike and pro-imperial (when he took an interest at all), and Wolsey as a man of peace, horrified by the cost of renewed warfare and working for a treaty with the French.[235] Such a distinction is not supported by the evidence, properly considered. Apart from misunderstanding the relationship between Wolsey and the king, such a view rests on a misunderstanding of the aims and complexities of diplomacy. First, Wolsey was no pacifist. In autumn 1523, as we have seen, it was Wolsey who advocated aggressive, offensive policies, not the king. It was Wolsey who when the campaign still seemed to be going well wrote to Henry that 'ther shalbe never such or like opportunite geven here after for the atteynyng of Fraunce'.[236] In the summer Wolsey had been above all concerned to avoid an expensive dribbling war that consumed treasure and won little — but by implication the right kind of war was acceptable.[237] That Wolsey's Christian humanist pacifism was largely rhetorical appears in his triumphant description in August 1523 of how Surrey was dealing with the Scots: Surrey has

so devastated and distroied al Tivedale and the Mershe, that ther is left neither house forteresse village tree catail corne or other socour for man; insomoche as somme of the people, whiche fled from the same and afterward retorned, fynding no sustentacion, were compelled to comme into England beggyng bred, whiche oftentymes whan they ete, they dye incontinently for the hungre passed; and with no emprisonment, kutting of thair eies, burnyng theym in the face, or otherwise can be kept awaye. Suche is the punishement of Almighty God to those, that be the disturbers of good peax, rest and quyete in Cristendome.[238]

Secondly, Wolsey was fully involved in military preparations and discussions of strategy and tactics. There is no sign of any flinching. Even in 1525, when what was done was small, Wolsey was discussing details of the projected campaign with the imperial commissioners, seeing to the appointment of Norfolk and captains, seeing to the raising of his own forces as bishop of Durham from the north, giving English ambassadors detailed instructions on what support they should secure from Margaret and the Netherlands.[239] Thirdly, Wolsey — and, as has been suggested above, Henry was in full agreement — took part in negotiations with the French between spring 1524 and March 1525 not because he wished to make peace above all

else, but because it was a prudent way of preserving English
interests — the king's honour and the security of the realm.
Seeking an insurance lest the French decisively defeated the
imperialists, or the imperialists and the French reached a truce
or a peace without consulting the English, was a sound
diplomatic manoeuvre. It should not be read as evidence of
Wolsey's supposed Francophilia. Fourthly, the evidence used
to support such an interpretation of Wolsey's foreign policy
rests on wrenching out of context remarks made in particular
circumstances. In late May 1525, for example, Wolsey wrote to
Henry, as we have seen, that there would be little benefit from
an English invasion of France, that the emperor would give
little or no assistance to Henry.[240] This letter was written after
the failure of the Amicable Grant and after receipt of
Sampson's pessimistic estimates of Charles' intentions. It must
not be used as evidence that Wolsey was opposed to an invasion
of France earlier, especially when the weight of evidence, as we
shall see, is that Wolsey was vigorously involved in demanding
the Amicable Grant which that planned invasion necessitated.
True, in January 1523 Wolsey had wished that Francis would
leave Italy in peace, and told the imperial ambassador that he
saw little likelihood that the English would ever conquer
France from Francis. But here Wolsey was playing hard to get
in an attempt to raise the level of assistance the English were
hoping to receive, and these comments were also made before
Bourbon's rebellion and its potential significance — which
dramatically influenced English policy in mid-1523 — were
fully grasped.

Notes

1 B[ritish] L[ibrary], Cotton MS, Cleopatra F vi. fos. 339^v–340 (H. Ellis,
   ed., *Original Letters [illustrative of English history]*, (11 vols. in 3 series,
   (1824–46), 3rd series, i. 373–4; J.S. Brewer, J. Gairdner and R.H.
   Brodie, eds., *L[etters and] P[apers] Foreign and Domestic, of the reign of Henry
   VIII]* (1862–1932), IV, i 1243).
2 *LP*, IV, i 1177 (cf. IV, i 481: Vives-Bishop Longland, 8 July 1524, in
   which Vives approvingly quotes the example of those in the islands of the
   new world, who, when war broke out, considered him most worthy of
   praise who desired peace and him least worthy who refused it).

3 BL, Cotton MS, Cleopatra F vi. fo. 350 (*LP*, IV, iii appendix 39).

4 *Ibid.*, Cleopatra, F vi fo. 337 (Ellis, *Original Letters*, 3rd series, i. 378; *LP*, IV i 1235).

5 BL, Cotton MS, Titus B i fo. 271ᵛ (*LP*, IV, i 1272).

6 E. Hall, *Chronicle* (1809 edn.), p. 695.

7 *Ibid.*, p. 661.

8 M.B. Davies, 'Suffolk's expedition to Montdidier, 1523', *Bulletin of the Faculty of Arts, Fouad I University*, vii (1944), pp. 33–43 at p. 41 [hereafter 'Griffith'].

9 Griffith, p. 37; Hall, *Chronicle*, pp. 663, 667, 669–70; *LP*, III, ii 3516, 3535.

10 Hall, *Chronicle*, p. 671.

11 Griffith, p. 41; cf. *LP*, III, ii 3580 on foot-soldiers' demands to return home.

12 G. Mattingly, ed., *Cal[endar of] S[tate] P[apers], Spanish, F[urther] S[upplement]*, (1947), p. 318.

13 Hall, *Chronicle*, p. 678.

14 *Ibid.*, p. 690.

15 *Ibid.*, p. 685.

16 *Cal. S.P., Spanish, F.S.*, pp. 369, 407.

17 Anonymous (?Cromwell's) speech in the commons, 1523: R.B. Merriman, *Life and Letters of Thomas Cromwell* (Oxford, 2 vols., 1902), i. 30–44 (*LP*, III, ii 2958).

18 Hall, *Chronicle*, p. 691.

19 P.J. Gwyn, 'Wolsey's foreign policy: the conferences at Calais and Bruges reconsidered', *Historical Journal*, xxiii (1980), pp. 755–72.

20 Hall, *Chronicle*, p. 655; *LP*, III, ii 2957, 2958; cf. Hall, *Chronicle*, p. 695 for similar claim in 1525.

21 *LP*, IV, i 1241, 1260; J.F. Larkin and P.L. Hughes, *Tudor Royal Proclamations* (3 vols., 1964–9), i. 137; cf. E. Searle and R. Burghart, 'The defence of England and the peasants' revolt', *Viator*, iii (1972), pp. 365–88.

22 *LP*, III, i 995; ii 1403.

23 *LP*, III, ii 2246, 2340, 2707, 2708, 2755, 2768, 2769, 2798, 2799, 2800, 2856, 2869, 2870, 2907, 2947, 2992, 3222, 3325, 3365, 3368, 3445, 3456.

24 *LP*, IV, i 317, 318, 324.

25 *LP*, IV, i 1131 etc.

26 P. Heath, 'The treason of Geoffrey Blythe, bishop of Coventry and Lichfield, 1503–31', *Bulletin of the Institute of Historical Research*, xlii (1969), pp. 101–09; *Cal. S.P., Spanish, F.S.*, p. 219.

27 *LP*, IV, i 68.

28 *LP*, III, i 1221.

29 *LP*, IV, i 2737.

30 *LP*, III, ii 2769.

31 *LP*, IV, i 243, 631.

32 *LP*, III, ii 2340.

33 *LP*, III, ii 2764; Hall, *Chronicle*, p. 655.

34 *LP*, IV, i 1167.

35 E.g. *Cal. S.P., Spanish, F.S.*, pp. 180, 233.
36 E. Armstrong, *The Emperor Charles V* (2 vols., 1910), i. 159.
37 *LP*, III, ii 2772, 2879; *Cal. S.P., Spanish, F.S.*, pp. 200, 206–7.
38 *LP*, III, ii 2772, 2773, 2879.
39 *Ibid.*, pp. 210–19; *LP*, III, ii 3064.
40 *Cal. S.P., Spanish, F.S.*, pp. 211, 215–17.
41 *LP*, III, ii 3064; *Cal. S.P., Spanish, F.S.* pp. 233–40.
42 R.J. Knecht, *Francis I* (Cambridge, 1982), pp. 148–58.
43 *Cal. S.P., Spanish*, ii no. 561 pp. 555–7; *LP*, III, ii 3149, 3150, 3225.
44 *State Papers [of Henry VIII]* (11 vols., 1830–52), vi. no. lviii p. 161 (*LP*, III, ii 3153). Cf. *Cal. S.P., Spanish, F.S.*, pp. 249, 245.
45 *Cal. S.P., Spanish, F.S.*, pp. 259–60; cf. *LP*, III, i 3203.
46 *State Papers*, vi. no. lv pp. 131–41 (*LP*, III, ii 3123); *Cal. S.P., Spanish, F.S.*, pp. 244, 249, 274.
47 *Cal. S.P., Spanish, F.S.*, pp. 208, 216, 220, 224–5, 242, 265, 267, 271, 273; *LP*, III, ii 3315, 3320.
48 *State Papers*, vi. no. lviii pp. 159–60 *(LP*, III, ii 3153).
49 *Cal. S.P., Spanish, F.S.*, p. 275.
50 *LP*, III, ii 3315.
51 *State Papers*, i no. lxxv pp. 135–40 (*LP*, III, ii 3346); cf. C.S.L. Davies, 'Supply services of English armed forces, 1509–1550', University of Oxford D.Phil. thesis, 1963, pp. 235–41.
52 *LP*, III, ii 3371, 3447, 3485; *Cal. S.P., Spanish, F.S.*, p. 275.
53 *State Papers*, vi. no. lxx pp. 202–4 (*LP*, III, ii 3601). For a full study of the campaign see S.J. Gunn, 'The duke of Suffolk's march on Paris in 1523', *English Historical Review* (forthcoming, 1986).
54 *Ibid.*, i. no. lxxviii p. 143 (*LP*, III, ii 3505).
55 Griffith, pp. 33–43; Hall, *Chronicle*, pp. 662–72.
56 *LP*, III, ii 3462; *Cal. S.P., Spanish, F.S.*, pp. 281, 284.
57 Hall, *Chronicle*, p. 662.
58 Griffith, pp. 34–5.
59 Hall, *Chronicle*, p. 668.
60 *Ibid.*; *LP*, III, 3378, 3485.
61 Hall, *Chronicle*, p. 670.
62 Griffith, pp. 38–9.
63 *State Papers*, vi. no. c pp. 347–8 (*LP*, IV, i 684).
64 Hall, *Chronicle*, p. 700; *Cal. S.P., Spanish, F.S.*, pp. 288–90; *LP*, IV, i 7.
65 *LP*, III, ii 3462.
66 *Cal. S.P., Spanish, F.S.*, pp. 281, 291; *LP*, III, ii 3498, 3525.
67 *LP*, III, ii 3601; appendix i. no. 392; *Cal. S.P., Spanish, F.S.*, pp. 283–4, 292; Hall, *Chronicle*, p. 671; *State Papers*, vi. no. lxx pp. 206–10; Knecht, *Francis I*, pp. 153–5.
68 Griffith, p. 39; *LP*, III, ii 3513.
69 Griffith, p. 39; Hall, *Chronicle*, p. 671; *Cal. S.P., Spanish, F.S.*, pp. 281, 285; Chatsworth, Clifford Letters no. 29 (6 Dec. 1523: fifth earl of Northumberland to eleventh lord Clifford: I owe this reference to Mr R.W. Hoyle); 6,927 soldiers were raised — 'so many souldiers which were appoyntted to haue gon over the see for the reenforsyng of the seid

army and afterward returned home from dyverse places as they were comyng up to London' (P[ublic] R[ecord] O[ffice], E/101/612/58): I am grateful to Mr S.J. Gunn for this reference).

70 *LP*, III, ii 3580; cf. *State Papers*, vi. no. lxx p. 204 (*LP*, III, ii 3601); *LP*, III, ii 3516; *Cal. S.P., Spanish, F.S.*, pp. 289–90; Hall, *Chronicle*, pp. 670–1; Griffith, pp. 6–7.

71 Hall, *Chronicle*, p. 671.

72 Griffith, p. 9.

73 *Ibid.*, pp. 9–11.

74 Hall, *Chronicle*, p. 672.

75 Chatsworth, Clifford Letters, no. 29.

76 *State Papers*, vi. no. lxxvi p. 233 (*LP*, IV, i 26).

77 *Cal. S.P., Spanish, F.S.*, p.291; *LP*, III, ii 3563, 3580, 3601; *State Papers*, vi. no. lxx p. 203.

78 *LP*, III, ii 2568.

79 *LP*, III, ii 2515.

80 *Cal. S.P., Spanish, F.S.*, p. 147.

81 *LP*, III, ii 2542.

82 *Cal. S.P., Spanish, F.S.*, pp. 271, 241–2, 269; *LP*, III, ii 3064, 3316, 3332.

83 *Cal. S.P., Spanish, F.S.*, pp. 281–2.

84 *Ibid.*, p. 283.

85 *Ibid.*, p. 291.

86 *LP*, IV, i 7.

87 *Cal. S.P., Spanish, F.S.*, pp. 282, 296, 299, 347; *LP*, III, ii 3462, 3532, 3533; IV, i 24; III, ii 3559. Margaret stressed to Charles on 7 April 1524 that an English invasion of France would assist the current Gelderland campaign by removing the threat of a French attack on Flanders and the consequent possibility that Buren's troops might have to leave Gelderland to defend Flanders, 'à tel peril de tous costez que povez considerer'. But she also admitted the impossibility of providing 3,000 horse and foot to support the English (Brussels AGR Etat et Audience 39 fo. 92^r: I owe this reference to Mr S.J. Gunn).

88 *Cal. S.P., Spanish, F.S.*, pp. 298–304.

89 *LP*, IV, i 30.

90 *LP*, IV, i 262, 356, 458, 478, 780.

91 *LP*, IV, i 186, 109, 110, 114, 224, 769; *Cal. S.P., Spanish, F.S.*, pp. 308, 329, 333.

92 *LP*, IV, i 186.

93 *Cal. S.P., Spanish, F.S.*, p. 318.

94 *Ibid.*, p. 328.

95 *Ibid.*, p. 340.

96 *Ibid.*, p. 346; *LP*, Appendix, i. 425.

97 Haus-, Hof- und Staatsarchiv, Vienna, PA 14/3/fos. 25^v, 32^r (I owe these references to Mr S.J. Gunn).

98 *Cal. S.P., Spanish, F.S.*, p. 350; *Cal. S.P., Spanish*, ii no. 654

99 *LP*, IV, i 438.

100 *Cal. S.P., Spanish, F.S.*, p. 362.

101 *Ibid.*, p. 311.

102 They would have been even more cautious had they been aware of the frank admissions of lack of money by Buren (in July: 'je ne scais bonnement ou l'on pourra trouver argent pour les gendarmes'), Margaret ('en extreme soussy' about how to pay for troops in September) and Charles (in October): Haus-, Hof- und Staatsarchiv, Vienna, PA 15/1/fos. 64ʳ, 184ʳ; 14/3/fo. 76ᵛ (I owe these references to Mr S.J. Gunn).

103 *Cal. S.P., Spanish, F.S.,* pp. 312–13, 318.

104 See below, p. 26.

105 Hall, *Chronicle,* pp. 673–82, 685–8 (p. 678 for Henry VIII); *LP,* IV, i 323, 334, 384, 414, 415, 418, 468, 469, 475, 479–80, 484, 564, 569, 591, 592, 734, 740, 749, 781.

106 See above, p. 8.

107 *LP,* IV, i 186.

108 *Cal. S.P., Spanish, F.S.,* p. 303.

109 *Cal. S.P., Spanish, ii* no. 618.

110 *Cal. S.P., Spanish, F.S.,* p. 319.

111 *LP,* IV, i 312, 313, 361, 362, 365, 379.

112 *State Papers,* vi, no. lxxxv pp. 262–4 (*LP,* IV, i 186). My italics.

113 *LP,* IV, i 365, 379.

114 *State Papers,* vi. no. lxxxix pp. 288–90 (*LP,* IV, i 374).

115 *LP,* IV, i 420, 441, 423, 455.

116 *State Papers,* vi. no. xciv p. 313 (*LP,* IV, i 442).

117 *LP,* IV, i 502.

118 *LP,* IV, i 589.

119 *LP,* IV, i 504, 552.

120 *LP,* IV, i 510.

121 *State Papers,* vi no. xcix pp. 333–4, 337–8 (*LP,* IV i 605).

122 *Cal. S.P., Spanish, F.S.,* pp. 385, 388–9, 391–3; cf. *State Papers,* vi, no. cix p. 400 (*LP,* IV, i 1083).

123 *Cal. S.P., Spanish, F.S.,* pp. 380, 376, 378–9.

124 *LP,* IV, i 605; *Cal. S.P., Spanish, F.S.,* pp. 378–9.

125 Hall, *Chronicle,* p. 684.

126 *State Papers,* iv. no. lviii pp. 120–1 (*LP,* IV, i 615). My italics.

127 *State Papers,* vi. no. c p. 346 (*LP,* IV, i 684).

128 *LP,* IV, i 570.

129 *LP,* IV, i 606.

130 *Cal. S.P., Spanish, F.S.,* pp. 392–3, 397; *LP,* IV, i 718, 724, 719, 751, 753.

131 *Cal. S.P., Spanish, F.S.,* p. 353.

132 *Ibid.,* pp. 329–35; *Cal. S.P., Spanish, ii.* no. 643; *LP,* IV, i 271–4.

133 *Cal. S.P., Spanish, F.S.,* p. 367; *State Papers,* vi. no. xcii p. 305 (*LP,* IV, i 394).

134 Deduced from *Cal. S.P., Spanish, F.S.,* pp. 367, 375, 378; *Cal. S.P., Spanish,* ii (i) no. 121 p. 211.

135 *Cal. S.P., Spanish, F.S.,* pp. 373–4.

136 Cf. *LP,* IV, i 841; *Cal. S.P., Spanish, F.S.,* pp. 401–2.

137 *Cal. S.P., Spanish, F.S.,* p. 410.

138 *Ibid.,* pp. 176, 182, 202; *LP,* III, ii 2881; R.G. Eaves, *Henry VIII's*

diplomacy 1513–1524: England's relations with the regency government of James V (New York, 1971). D.M. Head, 'Henry VIII's Scottish policy — a reassessment', *Scottish Historical Review*, lxi (1982), pp. 6–7 understates the potential threat that Albany posed.
139 *LP*, III, ii 3509, 3512.
140 *Cal. S.P., Spanish, F.S.*, p. 369.
141 *LP*, IV, i 117, 123, 144, 145, 396.
142 See *LP*, IV, i *passim;* ambassadors: *Cal. S.P., Spanish, F.S.*, pp. 426, 428–31; Hall, *Chronicle*, pp. 687–90; *Cal. S.P., Spanish*, iii (i) no. 1 pp. 4–5, no. 2 p. 17.
143 *Cal. S.P., Spanish, F.S.*, p. 421; *Cal. S.P., Spanish*, ii no. 703 p. 684; *LP*, IV, i 930–1.
144 *Cal. S.P., Spanish*, iii (i) no. 3 pp. 17–20; no. 7 pp. 26–7.
145 *LP*, IV, i 1069, 1018, 1036, 1083, 1152, 1153.
146 *Cal. S.P., Spanish, F.S.*, pp. 435, 437; *Cal. S.P., Spanish*, iii (i) nos. 9, 16, 17, pp. 36, 45–8.
147 *Cal. S.P., Spanish*, iii (i) no. 8 pp. 28–36; *Cal. S.P., Spanish, F.S.*, p. 435; *LP*, IV, i 1076, 1077.
148 *Cal. S.P., Spanish*, iii nos. 27, 33.
149 *State Papers*, vi no. cix pp. 391–3 (*LP*, IV, i 1083).
150 G. Jacqueton, *La politique extérieure de Louise de Savoie* (*Bibliothèque de l'école des hautes études*, lxxxviii (Paris, 1892), p. 81.
151 *State Papers*, vi no. lxxxv p. 277 (*LP*, IV, i 186).
152 *State Papers*, vi no. cix pp. 388–9 (*LP*, IV, 1083).
153 *Cal. S.P., Spanish, F.S.*, pp. 367–74, 388–94, 399, 421; *Cal. S.P., Spanish*, iii (i), no. 5 pp. 24–5.
154 *State Papers*, vi no. cix p. 395 (*LP*, IV, 1083).
155 Jacqueton, *Politique extérieure*, p. 59.
156 *Cal. S.P., Spanish, F.S.*, p. 435; *Cal. S.P., Spanish*, iii (i) nos. 3, 5 pp. 14, 23–5, 27.
157 Jacqueton, *Politique extérieure*, p. 306.
158 *Ibid.*, pp. 308–14 esp. pp. 308–11 (*LP*, IV, i 1160).
159 Hall, *Chronicle*, p. 693.
160 PRO SP1/33/fo. 163 (*State Papers*, i no. lxxxvi p. 158; *LP*, IV, I 1078); cf. *State Papers*, vi no. lxxxv pp. 262–3 (*LP*, IV, i 186).
161 *Cal. S.P., Spanish*, iii (i) no. 28.
162 K. Brandi, *The Emperor Charles V: the growth and destiny of a man and emperor* (1939), p. 219.
163 *Cal. S.P., Spanish*, iii (i) no. 33 p. 82.
164 R. Macquereau, *Histoire générale de l'Europe depuis la naissance de Charle-Quint jusqu'au cinq juin mdxxvii* (1765), p. 231.
165 Corporation of London Records Office, Letter Book N fo. 277; *Cal. S.P., Spanish*, iii (i) nos. 39, 43.
166 *Cal. S.P., Spanish*, iii (i) no. 39.
167 *State Papers*, vi no. cxiv pp. 417, 421, 424, 432–2 (*LP*, IV, 1212).
168 *LP*, IV, i 1301 (1).
169 Hall, *Chronicle*, p. 678.
170 *Ibid.*, pp. 694–5.

171 BL Cotton MS, Cleopatra F vi fo. 330 (*LP,* IV iii appendix 34).
172 Corporation of London Records Office, Letter Book N fos. 278–278ᵛ.
173 Hall, *Chronicle,* pp. 694–5.
174 *LP,* IV, i 1208, cf. 1283.
175 *Cal. S.P., Spanish,* iii (i) no. 39 pp. 86–8.
176 *Ibid.,* no. 43 p. 92.
177 *Ibid.,* nos. 39, 67, 75, pp. 87, 118, 125; *LP,* IV, iii appendix 32,
178 PRO SP1/34/fos. 114–15 (*LP,* IV, i 1249).
179 *LP,* IV, i 1261.
180 *Ibid.,* 1265.
181 *Ibid.,* 1262.
182 *LP,* IV, i 1301 (1), (2), 1307, 1312 (i and ii).
183 *LP,* IV, i 1289.
184 *Ibid.,* 1292.
185 *Ibid.,* 1169.
186 *Cal. S.P., Spanish,* iii (i) no. 86.
187 Ellis, *Original Letters,* 2nd series, i. 335 (*LP,* IV, i 2033).
188 *LP,* IV, i 1175.
189 *Ibid.,* 1283.
190 *Ibid.,* 1339.
191 *Ibid.,* 1357.
192 *Ibid.,* 1410.
193 *Cal. S.P., Spanish,* iii (i) no. 39 pp. 86–8.
194 *Ibid.,* no. 43 p. 92.
195 *Ibid.,* no. 61 pp. 108–12.
196 *Ibid.,* nos. 67, 70, 73, 75; pp. 118, 119, 122, 125.
197 *Ibid.,* no. 79.
198 *LP,* IV, i 1301.
199 Cf. *Cal. S.P., Spanish,* iii (i) no. 79.
200 See above, pp. 35–6 and n. 182.
201 *LP,* IV, i 1237.
202 *Ibid.,* i 1212 (2–9).
203 *State Papers,* vi no. cxiv pp. 412–36 (*LP,* IV i 1212); *LP,* IV, i 1249.
204 *LP,* IV, i 1250, 1255, 1264, 1271, 1296–7, 1378.
205 Brandi, *Charles V,* pp. 224–5; *Cal. S.P., Spanish,* iii (i) no. 52; *LP,* IV, 1213.
206 *LP,* IV, i 1189, 1190, 1203.
207 *Ibid.,* 1237, 1238.
208 *State Papers,* vi, no. cxv pp. 437–8 (*LP,* IV, i 1303).
209 PRO SP1/34/fo. 134 (*LP,* IV, i 1264). A year earlier, in March 1524, Wolsey had worried that nothing had come from Sampson since his letters of 12 and 24 November 1523 (*LP,* IV, 186).
210 *State Papers,* i no. lxxxviii p. 160 (*LP,* IV, 1371). The date of this letter — just 'Saturday' in the text — must be 27 May: (i) reference to decision of de Bèvres and Sauch to stay longer in England owing to the recent letters in code to which they did not have a cipher (*Cal. S.P., Spanish,* iii (i) nos. 97, 99 pp. 170–3); (ii) reference to sending of Spinnolus (Spinaloza/ Penalosa) by emperor (*Cal. S.P., Spanish,* iii (i) no. 111 pp. 190–1); (iii) reference to affairs of city and priory of Norwich (*LP,* IV, 1366).

211 *LP*, IV, i 1212 (1).
212 *Ibid.*, 780.
213 PRO SP1/34/fos. 114ᵛ–115 (Not in *LP*, IV, i 1249).
214 *Cal. S.P., Spanish*, iii (i) nos. 73, 79, 122, pp. 122, 134, 216–17.
215 *Cf. Cal. S.P., Spanish*, iii (i) nos. 86, 90 pp. 146, 153 and no. 97 p. 169; and no. 115.
216 *Cal. S.P., Spanish*, iii (i) no. 119.
217 Cf. remarks on the relationship between king and minister (in a different context) by R.B. Wernham, *English Historical Review*, lxxi (1956), pp. 92–5 at 95. It is very hard to see Wolsey as sole author of the plans of 1525, as some writers appear to do.
218 *Cal. S.P., Spanish, F.S.*, pp. 407, 403, 414.
219 *State Papers*, vi no. cix pp. 395–6 (*LP*, IV, i 1083).
220 P.J. Gwyn, 'Foreign policy 1515–1518', unpublished chapters of his forthcoming study of Cardinal Wolsey.
221 *Cal. S.P., Spanish, F.S.*, p. 388.
222 *LP*, III, ii 3405, 3421, 3531.
223 *State Papers*, i no. lxxiv p. 151 (*LP*, IV, i 882) (cf. *LP*, IV, 1018).
224 *LP*, III, ii 3571, 3578.
225 *State Papers*, i no. lxxxv p. 153 (*LP*, IV, 1063).
226 Hall, *Chronicle*, p. 691.
227 *Cal. S.P., Spanish, F.S.*, p. 374.
228 *Ibid.*, pp. 244, 246, 256, 259, 267, 278–80, 289, 291–2.
229 *Ibid.*, pp. 215–17.
230 *Cal. S.P., Spanish*, iii (i) no. 196.
231 *Cal. S.P., Spanish, F.S.*, p. 325.
232 *Ibid.*, p. 348.
233 Hall, *Chronicle*, pp. 671–2.
234 *Cal. S.P., Spanish*, iii (i) no. 79.
235 Cf. J.J. Scarisbrick, *Henry VIII* (1968) and (but far less sensitively) R.L. Woods, 'The Amicable Grant: some aspects of Thomas Wolsey's rule in England 1522–1526', University of California, Los Anglesles, Ph.D. thesis, 1974.
236 *State Papers*, i. no. lxxviii p. 143 (*LP*, III, ii 3505).
237 *State Papers*, vi. no. lviii pp. 159–60 (*LP*, III, ii 3513).
238 *State Papers*, vi no. lxi p. 173 (*LP*, III, ii 3281).
239 See above, pp.34–8.
240 *LP*, IV, i 1371. See n. 210 above.

2 The demands of 1525: war finance, rates, evolution of policy

Once the decision had been taken to prepare for an invasion of France in 1525, provided suitable imperial assistance was forthcoming, some financial demand was inevitable. It was beyond the capacity of any English monarch to finance wars, especially expensive invasions of France, from his own resources, that is from revenues from crown lands and customs duties, alone. In the later years of Henry VII's reign these amounted to some £40,000 p.a. each.[1] But the restricted campaign in France between 1488 and 1492 had cost £108,000,[2] the military ventures between spring 1511 and autumn 1514 cost £892,000 in wages, provisions and ordnance,[3] and the wars of the 1540s cost some £3.2m., of which one year (from September 1544 to September 1545) accounted for £560,000.[4] Henry and Wolsey were acutely aware of the financial constraints on military ambition. Asking parliament to grant taxes in 1523, Wolsey insisted that the defence to which the king was driven 'in no wise could be maintained without great somes of money'.[5] In doubting the wisdom of the strategy, ultimately adopted in autumn 1523, of seizing a number of French towns, Henry, according to Thomas More, thought 'that it wold be right hard for hym to fynd the money, that shold suffise to the continuall keping of his army so longe, both by see and by londe, namely so great as thobeteignyng of the townys shold requyre'.[6] In the middle of that campaign money nearly ran out. Wolsey implored the king 'that pitie it were they shulde, for lak or defaulte of money, be empeched' and called

on Henry 'for a tyme, to spare the somme of £10,000', to be
delivered to Sir Henry Wyatt in time to meet the next payment
due to Suffolk and his forces at the beginning of November.[7]
Earlier the likelihood of a 'great enterprise' with Charles
against the French had prompted the 'general proscription' of
1522, that remarkable survey intended to discover the military
might and the landed and mercantile wealth of the country. As
early as March 1522 Wolsey was intending to use this survey as
the basis of parliamentary taxation in support of the wars.[8] The
subsequent loans of 1522–3 and the subsidy voted in 1523 fall
unmistakably into the category of war finance. If a new
campaign were to take place in 1525, still more money would be
required. There is no evidence that there was any systematic
assessment of the state of royal finances in March 1525. News of
Pavia was sudden, time was pressing, the need obvious. The
council saw this at once: 'remembryng that it was determined,
that the kyng in proper persone should passe the sea, they
considered that aboue all thynges greate threasure and plentie
of money, must nedes be had in a readines'.[9] Writing of the
proposed invasion a month later, Bishop Tunstall implored 'I
pray almyghty god sende the kinges highnes fornishment of
money for the same'.[10] Archbishop Warham made the
connection between the invasion and the need for money
explicit, warning men in Kent of royal displeasure 'if his
subjectes shuld now, as far as in theym is, in not advauncyng
suche sommes as be demaunded, lett his Grace not to use this
opportunytie'.[11] It is misleading, however, to suppose that this
demand for money was merely a way of financing the normal
costs of government, even though some fears were expressed by
reluctant grantors that no invasion would be made. Nor is it
fitting to see the financial needs of 1525 as any novel 'crisis' or
as evidence of any 'structural breakdown' in English public
finance or the English polity. This difference between the
ordinary income of the crown and the increased expenditure
resulting from war was not new, nor especially worse in the
1520s than in earlier periods, although the dissipation in the
1510s of any inherited accumulated surpluses from the years of
peace would have by then made Henry's position more
difficult. Possibly warfare was becoming more expensive in the
early sixteenth century as armies grew in size, guns in number,

fortifications in complexity.[12] But it seems fairer to claim that wars always created financial problems: governments tend to fight wars, and when frightened, to prepare defences, right to the limits of their own and their country's resources.

Given that money was needed, it was necessary to determine how to raise it and at what rates. What Henry and Wolsey demanded in 1525 was always a grant, a non-refundable contribution, never, as is sometimes supposed, a loan that would be one day repaid, for example as a charge on future parliamentary taxation.[13] Only when Wolsey promised the Londoners that sums paid would be returned if the king did not cross over to France, or when Warham's instructions spoke of repayment if the French king recompensed Henry, could the request take on the appearance of a loan, but clearly the intention was that the money should be spent on a military campaign rather that it should ever be refunded.[14] The demand was to be administered in two stages. First, commissioners, 'the greatest men of euery shire',[15] (probably appointed generally on 21 March)[16] were to persuade those liable to acquiesce in a grant of a sum specified by the commissioners and based on the valuations made in 1522. No money changed hands at this point. It was this first stage that the commissioners were at when, with greater or lesser success, they were 'practising' people in April and early May 1525.[17] The second stage was to be that of payment: money was to be handed over to collectors ('with all diligence possible', possibly in two stages but wholly by Midsummer) who would in turn pass it over to the treasurer of the chamber.[18] But that stage, as we shall see, was never reached. Not a penny of the Amicable Grant was ever paid by anyone.[19] Technical confusions in the commissions — for example the commissioners of Norfolk received commissions covering the whole county rather than just the hundreds for which they were responsible — may be signs of haste.[20] It is important to note further that what was being demanded did not remain the same: the demands in mid-May were different from those of late March. Letters written, and comments made, in May must not, then, be taken as evidence of attitudes towards the original request.

The clergy were called upon to grant one-third of their yearly revenues or of the value of their movable goods if these were above £10, one-quarter if they were below £10.[21] No administrative document comparable to the instructions sent to Archbishop Warham, which gives these details, survives to show the rates demanded of the laity. Hall describes a sliding scale. Those worth £50 or more a year were to pay 3s. 4d. in the £, or one-sixth, those worth between £50 and £20 were to pay 2s. 8d. in the £, presumably an error for 1s. 8d. in the £, or one-twelfth, and those worth between £20 and £1 were to pay 1s. in the £, or one-twentieth. The commissioners made a distinction between those worth £20 and above and those worth less than £20, a line corresponding to one of the divisions on Hall's sliding scale. Elsewhere Hall uses the fraction one-sixth more generally, writing of demands of a sixth of every man's substance.[22] The duke of Norfolk's calculations suggest a rate of a sixth for those worth £20. He that paid £20 at the loan of 1522, Norfolk reported, had now granted £33 6s. 8d.; as the loan of 1522 had been at the rate of 2s. in the £, or one-tenth, that implies a rate of 3s. 4d., or one-sixth, in 1525.[23]

By the end of April the government was modifying its demands. There is no direct evidence of when or how this happened. Wolsey had already experienced difficulties in London and he and Henry had received reports from East Anglia and Kent and elsewhere of refusals on the grounds of poverty. It is possible that important decisions were taken when the dukes of Norfolk and Suffolk briefly returned to court from East Anglia to attend the king at the St George's Day celebrations, but this must remain speculative. Hall writes that when the commissioners sat in every shire 'the burden was so greuous, that it was denied, and the commons in euery place were so moued, that it was like to haue growen to a rebellion'. It was 'when this mischief was shewed to the kyng', Hall tells us, that Henry denied all knowledge of the demand (almost certainly, as we shall see, a lie), and then declared 'that he would demaunde no some certain, but suche as his louyng subiectes would graunt to hym of their good mindes toward the maintenaunce of his warres'. The king cancelled the demand for a sixth and replaced it by a request for a benevolence, that is a grant the size of which was left to the discretion of each donor. Hall says that the king 'sent his letters to the citee of London, and to all other places'.[24] Two such letters survive, sufficiently similar to indicate a circular letter. To the mayor and aldermen of London, Henry wrote on 25 April that from Wolsey he had heard of their good minds but also that their powers and abilities were not equal to those good minds. Because he did not desire their extreme impoverishment he had accordingly instructed Wolsey 'to shewe and declare vnto you what waies of moderacion we haue deuysed to be taken with you in this behalf'.[25] To the marquess of Dorset, commissioner in Warwickshire, Henry wrote that from his report he understood that although his subjects there were glad to strain themselves 'too do vnto vs all gratuite' possible, 'yet neuertheles their powars and abilites be not correspondent and equall vnto their good willes myndes and intencions, nor thei be able to make vnto vs payment of the sayed graunte with owt their extreme detryment and excessiue hinderaunce'. Not wishing his subjects to be overcharged and impoverished, Henry had sent 'instrucions wherin we haue declared our mynd and pleasur what wayes of moderacion we haue devised to be taken in this behalf'.[26] Clearly by 25 April Henry and Wolsey had decided to reduce the demand. Neither letter gives details of what those 'waies of moderacion' were; in London we know from Hall's account that the demand was changed to a request for a benevolence.

But the new policy does not seem to have been applied consistently. Rumours of concessions to London quickly spread and caused difficulties for commissioners elsewhere. Those in Kent reported that 'the common fame and brute of theis parteis is that the kinges hieghnes hath remytted the paymentes of such somes of money as were demaunded of the kinges graces subiectes of the Citie of London', adding 'which fame and brute as it is thought hath doon litle good here'.[27] In Norwich the duke of Norfolk noted that news had arrived on 29 April that Wolsey had spoken on 26 April with the mayor and twelve of the best of the city of London and had 'geven vnto them marvailous good wordies and had promised theim that they shuld pay noo more then they wold graunt of theire owne myndis'. These tidings, continued Norfolk, 'caused the maire and aldermen [of Norwich] . . . to desire me to vse theim in like maner'.[28] Evidently neither in Kent nor in Norfolk had the commissioners at the time of these letters — 3 May and 30 April respectively — been given instructions comparable to those that had been given to Wolsey to seek a benevolence. The duke of Norfolk had rather been trying to secure acquiescence in a grant of half of the original demand, that is one-twelfth instead of one-sixth. This may be deduced from his letter of 30 April. He was 'practising' the city of Norwich for a grant at this lower rate. When news came that Wolsey was conceding a benevolence in London, he tried out what would happen if the grant were similarly left entirely to the discretion of contributors in Norwich. The results were discouraging. 'Their graunte', he reported, 'shuld skante haue extendid to the vi[th] parte that the other was whan I was here laste', that is barely one-thirty-sixth. He therefore resorted to his earlier efforts to obtain a 'moiety' — a half of the original grant, that is one-twelfth — and could write 'nowe I truste this graunte at the leeste shalbee largely the oon half of thother'.[29] It is likely that before returning to East Anglia from London in late April Norfolk had been instructed, or had taken part in the making of the decision, to reduce the original demand from one-sixth to one-twelfth. What took him by surprise was news that Wolsey was conceding a benevolence. Norfolk and the duke of Suffolk expressed their concern at the confusion of policy when writing on 11 May (no doubt the more anxious after they had just subdued a rising, to which we shall return, in south Suffolk). If it were meant that people should pay more than they would grant of their good will, if, that is, a benevolence were to be sought generally, then they thought that their counties of Norfolk and Suffolk whose inhabitants had agreed to pay a moiety of the original demand would consider themselves hard done by. They did not doubt that Wolsey and the king would either order that 'suche a reasonable rate may bee appoynted vnyuersallie as bothe maye bee grauntid and paid' or else command 'suche sums to bee taken as the people of theire benyvolent mynde woll geve', which, they thought, 'shall extende to a right small some not only in theis parties but in all the realme'.[30] A day later, on learning more about the extent of the rebellion, the dukes wrote that whether Wolsey wanted them to continue practising for a moiety with those who had not yet granted or whether he wanted a general practice for a benevolence, they wished to defer it until they had spoken with him and the king. The confusion of policy is striking.[31]

What was happening in Kent only strengthens that impression. At a time when the Londoners were facing a request for a benevolence and the inhabitants of Norfolk and Suffolk were being dealt with for half the original demand, the commissioners of Kent assembled at Canterbury on 2–3 May were clearly practising with those worth £20 and above at the original rate.[32] Not until 5 May did Wolsey write to Archbishop Warham to tell him that royal demands had been reduced. The rate required from the clergy was lowered from one-third to one-sixth of their revenues, and the king had remitted 'to his commissioners and other his graces temporal subiectes of this his countie of Kent which haue made alre[ady] graunte half the sumes of money at the first sitting demaunded'. Kent was now being treated in the same way as Norfolk had been a little earlier: its lay inhabitants were being called upon to grant a moiety of the original demand, one-twelfth instead of one-sixth.[33] On 12 May Warham was ordered to defer practising with the clergy until the laity had been dealt with. He was to practise with groups of four, six or eight of the better sort of the laity to make the grant according to the new rate.[34] Despite the confusions, and the imprudent variations in what was being demanded, the government was still keen to raise some money. Wolsey pressed the Londoners hard on 26 April and 8 May. Henry sent a circular letter on 8 May urging commissioners who met with refusals to pay to proceed 'doucely' rather than by using violence in order to reform the refusers if possible.[35]

Then the final change came when Henry decided to abandon the demand altogether. According to Hall, this took place once the dukes of Norfolk and Suffolk brought the leaders of the rebellion with them to London and Henry assembled a great council. The king, in what has become a famous story, asked how it was that the commissions had been so straight, and then cancelled the demand, pardoning anyone who had openly or secretly refused it.[36] But this does not fit with the letters that the dukes sent to Wolsey and Henry, the latest of which was written on 17 May (and made it clear that the dukes would still be in East Anglia the following day). It is obvious from this last letter that the Amicable Grant had already been abandoned before the dukes returned to London. They acknowledged receipt of the king's letters dated 14 May: 'with as convenyent diligence as we may [we] shall notefie and cause to bee declared to the people his moste charitable and gracious mynde mencioned in his said lettre towardes theim'.[37] This letter surely contained the decision to revoke the demand. As on 12 May Wolsey had still been sending instructions on how to raise money to Warham, it can be deduced that Henry and Wolsey decided to abandon the Amicable Grant on 13 or 14 May.

This account of the implementation of the decision to seek a grant, and especially of the astonishing confusions of policy once the original demand was modified from late April, raises questions about the authorship of the scheme. Who was the author of the Amicable Grant? What were Henry's and Wolsey's intentions and actions in March to May 1525? Many historians have spoken of 'Wolsey's "Amicable Grant" ' and suggest that Henry was largely blameless: 'for once Henry's customary arrogation to himself of popular actions, which left to others the odium of unpopular ones, looks to have rested on the facts of the case'.[38] Yet the thrust of the discussion of foreign policy above has been that Henry and Wolsey worked as a team. In 1525 Henry's instinctive reaction to news of Pavia was to adopt an aggressive attitude and to prepare for an invasion of France, given necessary military support from the emperor. There is nothing to suggest that any of his counsellors, including Wolsey, disagreed. Once such a decision had been made, a renewed financial demand from the king's subjects became, as has been shown, inevitable. That background suggests that the Amicable Grant was the fruit of consensus among Henry, Wolsey and counsellors, rather than the policy of a single minister.

The principal source for any interpretation that places the responsibility for the Amicable Grant upon Wolsey and denies that Henry was involved is Edward Hall's *Chronicle*. But careful reading of Hall's account reveals a more complex situation. Hall describes two separate occasions which are relevant here. First, on hearing that refusals of the original demand of one-sixth were so great that they were thought likely to produce a rebellion, Henry 'saied that he neuer knewe of that demaunde' and substituted a benevolence.[39] Secondly, Hall relates how on learning of the rebellion in Suffolk, and after the dukes of

Norfolk and Suffolk had come to London, Henry told a great council which he had assembled that it had never been his intention to ask anything dishonourable or against his laws. 'Wherfore', he went on, 'he would know of whom it was long, that the commissions were so straight to demaunde the sixt parte of euery mannnes substaunce'. Wolsey 'excused himself' and then accepted the blame.[40] But neither of these instances remains so clear-cut on a closer examination. On the first occasion Hall describes how Wolsey claimed that it was he who persuaded Henry to reduce the demand: the king 'at my desire and peticion, was content to call in and abrogate the same commission'. Hall clearly intends his readers to treat this as a barefaced lie. It might be wiser to regard this whole episode, in which Hall's emphasis is on Wolsey's effrontery, with caution.[41] On the second occasion, Hall adds details which modify his principal argument against Wolsey. He relates how Wolsey defended himself by saying that when the question had been discussed in council, the king's counsellors, and especially the judges, had said the demand was lawful, a view confirmed by the churchmen. Wolsey only took on the responsibility 'because euery man laieth the burden from hym': he was content to accept it, 'and to endure the fame and noyes of the people for my goodwill toward the kyng, and comfort of you my lordes, and other the kynges counsailers', significantly adding, 'but the eternall God knoweth all'. Superficially read, Hall's account appears damning to Wolsey: closer attention shows inconsistencies, from which a more plausible conclusion would be that the Amicable Grant was indeed the responsibility of all, and not just one, of the counsellors.[42]

Hall also claimed that the commons blamed Wolsey for the demand. He tells us that the letters revoking it stated that Wolsey had not assented to the first demand which had, they continued, been devised by the lords and judges and other counsellors. It had rather been at Wolsey's petition and supplication that the king had cancelled the grant. 'The people toke all this for a mocke', says Hall, 'and saied God saue the Kyng, for the Cardinall is knowen well inough, the commons would heare no praise spoken of the Cardinall, they hated hym so muche'.[43] If Wolsey did indeed attempt, in such letters, to deny his involvement in the grant, it is not surprising that there was such a reaction. But there is no other evidence of such denials. There is, however, some evidence for popular accusations against Wolsey. Notes made in the 1640s for Lord Herbert, presumably from documents which no longer survive, state that the dukes of Suffolk and Norfolk wrote to Wolsey that the commons laid all the blame on him and that if any insurrection followed, the quarrel would only be against him.[44] In Griffith's chronicle, the spokesman of the rebels of southern Suffolk said it was their intention 'to go to his grace the king to complain of the Cardinal on account of the taxes which he set men one day after another to demand of them, though they had not the wherwithal to pay'.[45] There is one contemporary account on these lines. Warham reported that in Kent 'the people sore grudgeth and murmureth and spekith cursidly among theymselues as far as they dare; saying that they shall neuer haue rest of payments as long as some levithe', evidently intending Wolsey.[46] But these criticisms must be handled with circumspection. That Wolsey was blamed by the commons does not in itself prove that the king had nothing to do with the matter. Warham attempted to reassure Wolsey who had evidently been alarmed by the attacks reported against him: 'as touching yor grace it hath been and euer shalbe seen that who so euer be in most favor and most of counsell with a great prince shalbe maligned at and yll spoken of do he neuer so well'.[47] More directly, Wolsey himself answered these charges when replying to the dukes of Norfolk and Suffolk. 'It is the custome of the people when any thing miscontenteth them to blame those that be nerer about the king, and where they dare not vse there tongues against theyr sovereigne, they for coloring there malice will not fayle to giue evill tonguys against hym, howbeit, I am not sole and alone herein, etc'.[48] Not the least of the functions of chief ministers was to act as lightning conductors to draw away from their royal masters any resentments against unpopular policies: that is no reason for historians to be similarly distracted.

For there is much to suggest that Henry was aware of the Amicable Grant. Even Hall, in his inconsistencies, provides evidence for this. True, he writes that Henry 'saied that he neuer knewe of that demaunde' and that Henry 'thought it touched his honoure, that his counsaill should attempt suche a doubtfull matter in his name'. But Hall also spoke of Henry's claiming that 'some haue enformed me that my realme was neuer so riche, and that there should neuer trouble haue risen of that demaunde, and that men would pay at the first request'. Clearly Henry had at the very least been told of the plans and given some promises about the likely outcome. It is possible that Henry knew of and approved the general principle of the Amicable Grant but was not involved in the precise details. Hall's remark, 'wherefore by the Cardinall were deuised strange Commissions, and sent in thende of Marche to euery shire, and commissioners appoynted', could support such a view.[49] Those disaffected in Kent who 'denieth nott but they will give the Kings Grace according to thaire powres, but . . . woll in nowise geve at other mennys appointement whiche knowith not thaire neds' may have been protesting that the details of the demand had been drawn up ignorantly by Wolsey.[50] However this may be, there is much to suggest that Henry was involved throughout. The duke of Norfolk wrote 'howe I haue proceded and sped in suche besines as the kingis highnes sent me for into theis parties at this tyme' and that Suffolk and he had made arrangements 'to practice this graunte for the kingis highnes'.[51] Later Wolsey wrote to him that the king wished him to put the Amicable Grant in train: Norfolk responded that he was putting the king's commandment to good effect.[52] On 30 April, after the orginal demand had been reduced, Norfolk wrote to Wolsey that he had taken such order 'that I am in noo doubte the kinges highnes and your grace shalbee contentid with the graunte of this Shire'.[53] On 8 May Norfolk and Suffolk wrote directly to the king to report the disturbances in south Suffolk and to give him certain warnings. Significantly for any assessment of Henry's general involvement in the grant, they said that they had written several times to Wolsey 'whiche lettres we doubte not my said lord hath and doth shewe vnto yor highnes from tyme to tyme trusting yor grace wolbe contented that we write not to you of the circumstance as we do to hym, assuering your grace that we haue smalle leysour so to doo'.[54] They assumed that Henry was seeing all the news they were sending to Wolsey. A little later they asked Wolsey for clarification of the king's pleasure on an obscure point in recent instructions and mentioned 'his highnes formor lettres', implying some royal correspondence (which no longer survives).[55]

Letters to and from Archbishop Warham similarly suggest that Henry was fully involved. The disaffection that Warham reported on 5 April included much criticism of the king's foreign policy, linking that to the financial demands.[56] Reporting clerical reluctance to grant in his letter to Wolsey on 12 April, Warham noted that those from the monasteries which were just being suppressed grudged sorely at this new request. In his own comment Warham implied that while Wolsey was responsible for these dissolutions, it was the king who was the author of the Amicable Grant: 'whether it were better or not to spare the preceding ferther therin tyll this greate matier of the kinges grace be ended, I referr it to yor grace, albeyt it hath been thowght good policye in tymes past, not to broche to many matiers of displeasur at ons'.[57] Lecturing those who were refusing the grant, Warham made it plain that it was the king whom they were offending. Henry had a special trust in Kentishmen as he had been born in their county: now he had 'suche opportunitie as hath not been seen a long tyme'.[58] It is possible that the letters that Warham received from Sir Thomas Boleyn and Henry Guildford came directly from the king: both were important members of the royal household and Boleyn had certainly been attending the king in late March. When difficulties grew, Warham and the other commissioners in Kent wrote directly to the king (as Norfolk and Suffolk were to do).[59] On 8 May Warham acknowledged receipt of Wolsey's letter informing him of what he described as the king's reduction of the clerical demand. That reference to the king might be merely formal. But it need not be. Warham wished to have it confirmed that this reduction also applied to him and so he appealed to Wolsey to ask this of the king. 'I trust and so humbly beseche yor grace to be mediator for me to his highnes that in consideration of my charges and peynes in his graces causes susteyned by his graces commaundement I for my parte maybe in no worse condition than any of his graces said commissioners or subiectes be'.[60] And when Warham got the confirmation he sought he thanked Wolsey for being a mediator to the king for him. It would be quite rash to dismiss all this as rhetoric and to suppose that Henry played no part in any of these decisions.[61] Cavendish's story of how in the late 1520s Anne Boleyn tried to do down Wolsey in Henry's eyes by dwelling on 'what debt & danger the Cardynall hathe brought you in with all yor subiectes', referring to the loan of 1522–3, is relevant to any assessment of Henry's role in the making of financial policy: Henry replied 'well, well . . . as for that ther is in hyme no blame for I knowe that matter better than you or any other'.[62]

Wolsey and Henry were in contact during the period of the Amicable Grant. King and cardinal were together in early March, co-ordinating their response to the newly arrived ambassadors from Flanders,[63] and they were together after news of Pavia arrived. Both attended the service of celebration in St Paul's on 12 March.[64] It does seem that they were then apart: Wolsey was at Bridewell, Henry at Greenwich.[65] In late March Wolsey wrote to Henry that he would like to see him, and then confirmed this. On 1 April he had received from Sir Thomas Boleyn

your gracious tokyn by whom I haue also understande that in case ye were aduertysed by me that yor comyng and beyng here [Westminster?] might be to thadvauncement of yor affaires ye woulde refuse no labour ne payne so to doo. Verely sir there can be no thing in myne opinion more to the furtheraunce and spedy execution of yor causis than yor beyng in such places wher I mought from tyme to tyme commodiously repair vnto yor presence for the knowledge of yor advise counsaile and pleasure in such matiers as be dayly occurrent and emergent. Wherfor if it shall please yor grace to take the payne to come to this my poor howse the same shall not onely be to the settyng forth of yor said causis but also to me singular rejoysyng consolacion and comfort.[66]

This is not the letter of a minister confidently and happily acting independently of his master. Henry and Wolsey certainly met on 11 or 12 April, and possibly earlier on 7 April, at Greenwich.[67] Wolsey was back with the king at Greenwich on 18 April when both received the imperial ambassadors.[68] It is inconceivable that Henry did not discuss the Amicable Grant with Wolsey during their meetings in mid-April. There may well have been a broader discussion when the dukes of Norfolk and Suffolk attended the king on St George's Day.[69] Thereafter there is little evidence that Henry and Wolsey met. Wolsey spent late April and early May at Hampton Court, returning to

London on 15 May, while Henry was at Windsor by 14 May.[70] But lack of evidence cannot be conclusive. It is tempting to ascribe the confusion of policy in these weeks to the lack of contact between king and minister: this would also explain the desire of Norfolk and Suffolk for a council. But this is speculative. What remains difficult to accept, on the basis of the information of Wolsey's and Henry's movements, is that Henry was ignorant of the Amicable Grant. It is just possible to argue that Wolsey was acting without much consultation in drawing up commissions in late March, but his letter of 1 April suggests that he was reluctant to take decisions on the king's behalf. Moreover Henry was very much kept informed when Wolsey's negotiations with the imperial commissioners were leading nowhere in mid-April. Obviously the evidence is incomplete and ambiguous but it seems most plausible to see Wolsey as the chief executive of the Amicable Grant, directing it in detail and from day to day, and Henry as the chairman, maintaining overall supervision and taking part in the principal decisions.

But such an interpretation would be challenged, and modified, by those who far from seeing Wolsey as the sole author of the demand, think that he was unenthusiastic or, in another version, that he deliberately sabotaged the venture. Such charges begin by taking Wolsey as a pacifist, a view of him that has already been questioned. He is seen as hostile to the proposed invasion of France in 1525, which is regarded as the desire of the king and nobility rather than of the cardinal. Here interpretations diverge. One set of charges runs thus. Wolsey was not keen on the war, unenthusiastic about the Amicable Grant, and therefore seized on refusals and opposition in order to persuade the king first to reduce, and then to cancel, the grant, and with its failure, to abandon the projected invasion.[71] A stronger line puts forward a remarkable picture of Wolsey as arch-manipulator. He deceived Henry and did the best he could deliberately to wreck the planned invasion. He quite purposefully set the demands at an impossibly high rate, fully expecting that this would provoke refusals and rebellions. In order to discredit his alleged rivals the dukes of Norfolk and Suffolk and their warlike policy, he sent them as commissioners into their 'countries', confident that the impossible duty imposed upon them would both show them how illusory their dreams were and, as they faced disturbances, undermine their local power, so diminishing them and their policy in the eyes of the king. By making concessions to London at a crucial point, Wolsey further weakened their position. He then cemented his triumph by prevailing on Henry to remit the grant and give up a bellicose foreign policy.[72] Much of this second argument is simply implausible. Would a chief minister, especially one who was solidly established, as Wolsey was in 1525, risk, or stir up, a rebellion (which, after all, could have become much more serious) to do down supposed rivals (which may well, as will be suggested below, be to find conflict where none existed)? Both arguments can be rebutted by an analysis of Wolsey's actions during the Amicable Grant.

On Hall's account Wolsey was vigorously enforcing the demand in London, the area of his commission. He met the mayor, Sir William Bailey, aldermen and divers head commoners, forcefully presented royal claims to France and threateningly demanded contributions. He then saw commoners daily, imprisoning some of them for their words to him. Once the original demand was reduced in late April, Wolsey again received the leaders of London and urged them to grant a benevolence. On 8 May he told them he would examine everyone individually, denied the validity of an act of parliament against benevolences passed in Richard III's reign, and threatened that the king would 'come with strong power them to oppresse' if the commons did anything against the mayor.[73] It is true that the city thanked Wolsey 'for his good and gracious mediacion made to the king' in late April[74] but it would be wrong to take this at face value as proof of Wolsey's reluctance to enforce the grant, given what else we know of Wolsey's attitude towards London. Hall does maintain that Wolsey made the best of the concessions both when the original demand was reduced and when the whole grant was abandoned, but this must be treated with caution as evidence of Wolsey's motives. On 26 April Wolsey, according to Hall, told the mayor and aldermen that he had informed the king how willingly the city had granted (as Hall goes on to say, a lie), despite their great losses and charges, but that 'then I kneled doune to his grace, shewyng hym both your good myndes towarde hym, and also the charges, that you continually sustein', who 'at my desire and peticion' was content to call in the commission and ask instead for a benevolence. Hall did not intend this to be taken as evidence of Wolsey's reluctance to enforce the Amicable Grant: on the contrary he asks the reader 'here note', that if the cardinal had not said that the first demand had been pardoned, they would have answered him that they never agreed to that demand, 'and for a suretie no more they did not', and that the citizens held their peace 'sore grudgyng at the liuyng of the Cardinal, and openly saying that he was the verie cause and occasion of this demaunde, and would plucke the peoples hartes from the kyng'.[75] On 19 May Wolsey sent for the mayor, aldermen and certain commoners and told them that 'at my humble request' the king had pardoned them of the sums demanded them. In Hall's account this follows his description of the royal revocation of the demand for which Wolsey stood blamed and of how in letters to commissioners it was claimed (falsely and incredibly, Hall implies) that Wolsey had never assented to the first demand. Again Hall in no way intends his reader to suppose that Wolsey had persuaded the king to abandon the grant. He rather shows Wolsey still trying to salvage something for the future, asking the Londoners to accept the pardon by agreeing 'that you be the kynges, bodie and goodes at his will and pleasure'. Hall intends to show Wolsey as responsible for the Amicable Grant, that he vigorously and despotically pursued the demand, that when the demand was reduced and then abandoned he claimed to have been the suitor to the king for the relief of the people, a claim that Hall presents as duplicity.[76] While some inconsistencies suggest that royal involvement was greater than Hall allows, as has been argued above, nothing here shows that Wolsey was anything but full square behind the grant. There is no sign that he relented before the king did or that he was half-hearted in the prosecution of the demand. Of course Hall is neither an unbiased nor a consistent witness but it is vital not to base an interpretation on quotations from his *Chronicle* drawn out of context and used against his intentions without any attempt to justify such use.

What does surviving correspondence show of Wolsey's attitude towards the grant? Does he emerge as vigorous in his enforcement or are there hints of lack of enthusiasm? How strict do the letters show him to be in his dealings with those who refused to grant? Those reports by Warham in which Wolsey was blamed for the demand itself, while more uncertain evidence than a superficial glance would suggest, do hint that Wolsey's role was visible. Even if the commons were blaming an evil counsellor for a policy that was as much the king's as the counsellors', it is still significant that Wolsey was singled out: would this have happened if there were any suspicion that Wolsey was sympathetic to the refusers? The details and, more importantly, the tone, of the letters to and from Warham suggest that Wolsey was seriously concerned to raise money and in no way favoured resistance. He was clearly displeased at popular criticism, judging from the lengths to which Warham thought it worth going to soothe his feelings.[77] (If this might still be seen as evidence of Wolsey's deviousness — he was especially unhappy to be criticised for a policy he did not support — it does at least indicate that his policy was misfiring to the point of drawing popular ill-will against him, as well as against those whom he wished to discredit.) Warham's letter to Wolsey on 15 April reporting clerical disaffection does not suggest that he expected Wolsey in any way to welcome his difficulties: he urged strong action against lay refusers.[78] True, Wolsey ordered Warham to postpone an assembly of the clergy, but it would be rash to charge Wolsey with partiality towards the clergy and a willingness to see them excused from the demand on such evidence.[79] The tone of the letters of the Kent commissioners in early May strongly hints that they would prefer not to assemble those worth less than £20 but the letters also make it plain that they were still being expected to do so by Wolsey and the king.[80] Warham's acknowledgment of Wolsey's letter of 5 May informing him that the king had reduced the demand from the clergy and laity by half does not show that Wolsey was the instigator of that concession. Warham's language rather suggests that he saw such decisions as the king's, and Wolsey as an important influence, as a mediator.[81] It is important here not to misread Warham's report on 12 May that despite the concessions, the laity were still saying things they should not. 'Surely it apperith by the same', wrote Warham, referring to the reduction, 'that yor grace is very singular good mediator for the commons to the kinges highnes, and that they be muche more bounden to yor grace than they haue witte or reason to consider, God knoweth ther is an indiscrete and inordinate multitude of theym which at euery light fleeyng tale be inclined and kendled to il imaginations inuentions and ill attemptates rather than to good'. This shows *not* that Wolsey disliked the Amicable Grant, *not* that he was the sole author of its reduction, but that, despite that concession, the commons were still attacking him as they had in April, behaving (in Warham's eyes) unfairly and badly. Moreover Warham's letter shows that Wolsey was still determined to secure some money from the laity of Kent. He wanted Warham to gather the better sort in groups of four, six or eight and 'practise' with them. Warham was much more doubtful about the prospects of success by such methods and anxious about the risk of unlawful assemblies.[82] In Wolsey's dealings with Kent there is no case to be made that he was lenient.

Wolsey was similarly vigorous in prosecuting the grant in East Anglia. He apparently misunderstood some of the duke of Norfolk's actions in early April and accordingly rebuked him sharply. He thought that Norfolk had made a great mistake in agreeing that the inhabitants of Norfolk should not be liable if other counties were not: Norfolk had simply seen this as a sensible means of persuasion. What is notable here is that Wolsey was anxious for the success of the grant. Again Wolsey voiced surprise that there were so few wealthy men in Norwich: Norfolk insisted that his return was correct and offered to pay the difference himself if it were later found to be wrong. Wolsey was clearly keen that the grant should raise the largest possible sums.[83] It is simply wrong to say that Wolsey wished to keep Norfolk and Suffolk in their 'countries' to rub their faces in the mud of resistance: he fully expected Norfolk to be back at court soon, and both dukes did attend the St George's Day celebrations.[84] Nor was the use of magnates to supervise financial demands unusual: they had been involved in the loan of 1522–3. When Norfolk and Suffolk, facing rebellion, recommended on 8 May that if there were outbreaks in other counties, Wolsey should 'by yor greate and high wisdome doo attempt with some dulce meanes to tempre their madnes and vntrouth', they were implying not that Wolsey was being lenient but that he might react too harshly.[85] And Wolsey did indeed instruct them to be firm with the rebels around Lavenham, and make a fearful example to others: as they had not submitted till force was levied against them, they should now be more sharply punished than if they had come in earlier. Norfolk and Suffolk insisted that they had been severe and defended themselves to Wolsey against apparent charges that they had been too lenient.[86] In the letters to and from Norfolk and Suffolk, then, Wolsey emerges determined and firm. It may be, of course, that the severity against rebels recommended by the minister in fact reflects Henry's habitual harshness towards what he saw as treason, but there is no sign that Wolsey was in any way unhappy to urge on such a policy.

If Wolsey vigorously pursued the Amicable Grant, was he nonetheless responsible for the decision to reduce, and then to cancel, the demand? There is no direct evidence, as we have seen, for the making of the decision to reduce the grant. Wolsey, according to Hall, tried to take credit, but Hall and the Londoners were disbelieving. The letters to the mayor of London and the marquess of Dorset informing them of the ways of moderation now being pursued were signed by the king. Does this suggest at least some royal involvement? Did some sort of conference including the dukes of Norfolk and Suffolk take place around St George's Day? Might a reduction have been decided upon in principle then and perhaps left to commissioners' discretion thereafter? No doubt Wolsey advised but surely it was the volume of dissatisfaction reported by commissioners, and not some ministerial complaisance, that persuaded the king and his counsellors to relent. According to Hall, Wolsey claimed that he had influenced the king's cancellation of the demand, but Hall certainly did not intend this to be believed. Wolsey's letter to Norfolk and Suffolk, written after the cancellation, was concerned with the punishment of rebels and apparently made no mention of any part he may have played in it. It was Henry's letters of 14 May, not Wolsey's, that informed them of the end of the demand. Moreover even if some evidence could be produced to show that in mid-May Wolsey did favour abandoning the enterprise, it would be rash to go on to argue that Wolsey had always opposed it. A much more likely explanation is that the rebellion in south Suffolk, continuing tensions in London, and difficulties and resistance elsewhere made Henry and Wolsey, and no doubt other counsellors, realise that the Amicable Grant had become impossible: the political risks and costs had become too great. Policy evolved according to news of opposition: first, a relaxation of the original demand (amid some confusion and inconsistency) in late April, then a realisation that opposition was too great even for a reduced request. In this there is no need to see Henry and Wolsey as in any way opposed to each other or as following separate policies.

Notes

1 B.P. Wolffe, *The Crown Lands 1461–1536* (1970), p. 69; B.P. Wolffe, 'Henry VII's land revenues and chamber finance', *English Historical Review*, lxxix (1964), p. 252; W.G. Hoskins, *The Age of Plunder* (1976), pp. 181–2.
2 R.S. Schofield, 'Parliamentary lay taxation, 1485–1547', University of Cambridge Ph.D. thesis, 1963, p. 431 n.1; p. 9 n.16.
3 F.C. Dietz, *English Government Finance 1485–1641 vol. i 1485–1558* (2nd edn., 1964), p. 91.
4 Schofield, thesis cit., p. 431 n.1; Davies, thesis cit., pp. 242, 338.
5 Hall, *Chronicle*, p. 655.
6 *State Papers,* i no. lxxv p. 138 (*LP,* III, ii 3346).
7 *State Papers,* i no. lxxix p. 144 (*LP,* III, ii 3433).
8 *Cal. S.P., Spanish., F.S.,* p. 99; J.J. Goring, 'The general proscription of 1522', *English Historical Review*, lxxxvi (1971), pp. 681–705.
9 Hall, *Chronicle*, p. 694.
10 PRO SP1/34/fo. 134 (*LP,* IV, i 1264).
11 B.L. Cotton MS, Cleopatra F vi fo. 347 (Ellis, *Original Letters*, 3rd series, i. 361; *LP,* IV, v 1266).
12 Davies, thesis cit., pp. 1–4.
13 Those who describe it as a loan include G.R. Elton, *The Tudor Constitution* (2nd edn., Cambridge, 1982), p. 44; R.L. Woods, 'Individuals in the rioting crowd: a new approach', *Journal of Interdisciplinary History*, xiv (1983), p. 1; P.A. Clark, *English provincial society from the Reformation to the Revolution: religion, politics and society in Kent 1500–1640* (Hassocks, 1977), p. 21.
14 Hall, *Chronicle*, pp. 699, 701; *LP,* IV, iii appendix 34.
15 Hall, *Chronicle*, p. 694.
16 *LP,* IV, i 1199, 1200.
17 B.L. Cotton MS, Cleopatra F vi fos. 336–8 (Ellis, *Original Letters*, 3rd series, i. 376–81; *LP,* IV, i 1235) is a vivid example.
18 PRO SP1/34/fo. 143 (*LP,* IV, i 1284); *LP,* IV, iii appendix 34.

19 Those who say that money was paid include Woods, *loc. cit.*, p. 1; Clark, *English provincial society*, p. 21.
20 *LP*, IV i 1295; cf. IV, i 1272.
21 B.L. Cotton MS, Cleopatra F vi fo. 330 (*LP*, IV, iii appendix 34); B.L. Cotton MS, Titus B i fos. 273–273ᵛ (*LP*, IV, i 1267); PRO SP1/234/fo. 240 (*LP*, appendix 457); Hall, *Chronicle*, p. 696. Puzzlingly the instructions for Warham claim that although these rates may seem great, the sums raised would amount to less than the loan of 1522: as that had been levied at the rate of one-quarter, not one-third, of higher yearly revenues, this claim would not be true. (B.L. Cotton MS, Cleopatra F vi fo. 330 (*LP*, IV, iii appendix 34.)
22 Hall, *Chronicle*, pp. 694, 696, 700; B.L. Cotton MS, Cleopatra F vi fo. 323 (*LP*, IV, iii appendix 36). Cf. *LP*, IV, i 1305, 1306, 1311.
23 B.L. Cotton MS, Cleopatra F vi fo. 323 (*LP*, IV, iii appendix 36).
24 Hall, *Chronicle*, p. 697.
25 Corporation of London Records Office, Letter Book N fos. 278–278ᵛ; for acknowledgement and a request for a delay of 14 days to 12 May, see Letter Book N fo. 279; Journal 12 fo. 331ᵛ.
26 Coventry Record Office, A 79 i p. 55, cited by C. Phythian-Adams, *Desolation of a city: Coventry and the urban crisis of the late middle ages* (Cambridge, 1979), pp. 63, 254 (I am most grateful to Mr D.J. Rimmer, city archivist, for a copy of this document).
27 PRO SP1/34/fo. 173 (*LP*, IV, i 1306); SP1/34/fo. 185ᵛ (*LP*, IV, i 1311).
28 PRO SP1/34/fo. 164 (*LP*, IV, 1295).
29 *Ibid.*
30 B.L. Cotton MS, Cleopatra F vi fos. 325–326ᵛ (Ellis, *Original Letters*, 3rd series, ii. 3–7; *LP*, IV, i 1323).
31 PRO SP1/34/fo. 96 (*LP*, IV, i 1329).
32 PRO SP1/34/fo. 185 (*LP*, IV i 1305, 1306, 1311).
33 PRO SP1/234/fos. 240–240ᵛ (*LP* appendix 457).
34 B.L. Cotton MS, Cleopatra F vi fo. 341 (Ellis, *Original Letters*, 3rd series, ii. 8–9; *LP* IV, i 1332).
35 Bodleian Library, Oxford, MS Jesus c. 74 fo. 317 (*LP*, IV, i 1318). (I am grateful to Mr P.J. Gwyn for informing me of the location of this MS.)
36 Hall, *Chronicle*, pp. 700–1.
37 PRO SP1/34/fo. 209 (*LP*, IV, i 1343).
38 E.g. G.R. Elton, *England under the Tudors* (1955), p. 78 ('only Henry's personal intervention saved the situation'); *Reform and Reformation* (1977), pp. 90–1 (quotation in text, and 'the king began to hear what was happening; threatened with a serious attack upon the peace of the realm, he showed himself possessed of better political sense than his chancellor [Wolsey]'); (in both these the date is given as 1524); *The Tudor Constitution* (Cambridge, 1st edn., 1960, 2nd edn., 1982), pp. 43/44; J.J. Goring, 'The riot at Bayham Abbey, June 1525', *Sussex Archaeological Collections*, cxvi (1978), p. 4.
39 Hall, *Chronicle*, p. 697.
40 *Ibid.*, pp. 700–1.
41 *Ibid.*, p. 698.

42 *Ibid.*, p. 700.

43 *Ibid.*, p. 701.

44 Bodleian Library, MS Jesus c. 74, fo. 317 (*LP*, IV, i 1318).

45 *Historical Manuscripts Commission, manuscripts in the Welsh language* [hereafter *HMC, Wales*], 48th appendix, part i, p. iv. (I am most grateful to Mr P.J. Gwyn for this reference.)

46 B.L. Cotton MS, Cleopatra F vi fo. 339 (Ellis, *Original Letters*, 3rd series, i. 371; *LP*, IV, i 1243).

47 B.L. Cotton MS, Cleopatra F vi fo. 350ᵛ (*LP*, IV, iii appendix 39).

48 Bodleian Library, MS Jesus c. 74 fo. 317 (*LP*, IV i 1318).

49 Hall, *Chronicle*, pp. 697, 700–1, 694; cf. Scarisbrick, *Henry VIII*, p. 139.

50 B.L. Cotton MS, Cleopatra F vi fo. 339 (Ellis, *Original Letters*, 3rd series, i. 373; *LP*, IV, i 1243).

51 B.L. Cotton MS, Cleopatra F vi fo. 336 (Ellis, *Original Letters*, 3rd series, i. 376; *LP*, IV, 1235); PRO SP1/34/fo. 131 (*LP*, IV i 1241).

52 B.L. Cotton MS, Caligula E iii fo. 4 (*LP*, IV, 1261); B.L. Cotton MS, Cleopatra F vi fo. 323 (*LP*, IV, iii appendix 36).

53 PRO SP1/34/fo. 164 (*LP*, IV, i 1295).

54 PRO SP1/34/fo. 190 (*LP*, IV, i 1319).

55 B.L. Cotton MS, Cleopatra F vi fos. 325ᵛ–6 (Ellis, *Original Letters*, 3rd series, ii. 6–7; *LP*, IV, i 1323); PRO SP1/34/fo. 209 (*LP*, IV, i 1343).

56 B.L. Cotton MS, Cleopatra F vi fos. 339ᵛ–40 (Ellis, *Original Letters*, 3rd series, i. 371–4; *LP*, IV, i 1243.

57 PRO SP1/34/fo. 145 (*LP*, IV, i 1263).

58 B.L. Cotton MS, Cleopatra F vi fo. 347 (Ellis, *Original Letters*, 3rd series, i. 360; *LP*, IV, i 1266.

59 *LP*, IV, i 1305, 1311.

60 PRO SP1/234/fo. 240ᵛ (*LP*, appendix 457).

61 B.L. Cotton MS, Cleopatra F vi fo. 341 (Ellis, *Original Letters*, 3rd series, ii. 8; *LP*, IV, i 1332).

62 R.S. Sylvester, ed., *The Life and Death of Cardinal Wolsey*, Early English Text Society, ccxliii (1959), p. 95.

63 *Cal. S.P., Spanish,* iii (i) no. 33 p. 77.

64 *Ibid.*, no. 43 p. 91.

65 *LP*, IV, i 1200, 1222, 1224.

66 *LP*, IV, i 1234.

67 *Cal. S.P., Spanish,* iii (i) no. 73 p. 121; *LP*, IV, i 1261, 1262, 1264.

68 *Cal. S.P., Spanish,* iii (i) no. 79 pp. 135–6.

69 J. Anstis, ed., *The register of the most noble order of the garter* (2 vols., 1724), i. 367–9.

70 Hall, *Chronicle*, p. 698; *Cal. S.P., Spanish,* iii (i) nos. 86, 90, 97 pp. 145, 164, 169; *LP*, IV, i 1343; appendix 457.

71 Scarisbrick, *Henry VIII*; D.M. Head, 'The life and career of Thomas Howard, third duke of Norfolk: the anatomy of Tudor politics 1473–1554', Florida State University Ph.D. thesis, 1978, p. 187.

72 R.L. Woods, 'The Amicable Grant: some aspects of Thomas Wolsey's rule in England, 1522–1526', University of California, Los Angeles, Ph.D. thesis, 1974, esp. chs. iv and v.

73 Hall, *Chronicle*, pp. 694–9.
74 Corporation of London Records Office, Letter Book N fo. 279 (though letter itself from king).
75 Hall, *Chronicle*, p. 698.
76 *Ibid.*, p. 701. J. Kennedy ('The city of London and the crown c.1509–c.1529', University of Manchester M.A. thesis, 1978), whose main line is that Wolsey acted as patron of the city of London, mediating between the king and the city, nonetheless sees Wolsey as here putting the king's interests first (p. 180).
77 B.L. Cotton MS, Cleopatra F vi fo. 350 (*LP*, IV, iii appendix 39).
78 B.L. Cotton MS, Titus B i fo. 274 (*LP*, IV, i 1267).
79 B.L. Cotton MS, Cleopatra F vi fo. 350 (*LP*, IV, iii appendix 39).
80 *LP*, IV, i 1305, 1306, 1311.
81 PRO SP1/234/fo. 240 (*LP*, appendix 457).
82 B.L. Cotton MS, Cleopatra F vi fos. 341–341ᵛ (Ellis, *Original Letters*, 3rd series, ii. 9–10; *LP*, IV, 1332). For a different reading, of Wolsey as persuading the king to relent, see Scarisbrick, *Henry VIII*, p. 139.
83 B.L. Cotton MS, Cleopatra F vi fos. 323ᵛ–324 (*LP*, IV, iii appendix 36).
84 B.L. Cotton MS, Caligula E iii fo. 4 (*LP*, IV, 1261).
85 PRO SP1/34/fo. 190 (*LP*, IV, i 1319).
86 B.L. Cotton MS, appendix L fo. 12 (*LP*, IV, 1324).

3   The dukes of Norfolk and Suffolk and the Amicable Grant

What was the attitude of the dukes of Norfolk and Suffolk to the Amicable Grant? Did they deliberately provoke refusals and disturbances, or did they capitalise on troubles which had occurred spontaneously in order to do down Wolsey? Or did they discharge their duties loyally and skilfully despite considerable and increasing difficulties?

The duke of Norfolk was sent to East Anglia in late March. Nothing in his first letter to Wolsey suggests that he was anything but a keen and efficient administrator. On his way he had ordered the sheriff of Norfolk to assemble selected gentlemen at Norwich on 29 March. From Kenninghall on 1 April he reported how he had first broken the matter to six or seven of the wisest men of the shire, then the next day to a further six or seven, and finally to the remainder. All had been persuaded to agree to the demand; all had signed a bill in their own hands indicating the rate at which they were to pay. These men were to serve as commissioners in the county. Norfolk gave them the books of assessments that had been made for the loan of 1522 and divided up the hundreds of the county between them. He also arranged publicity: fires were to be lit in every town, discreet persons were appointed to declare to the people that the French king had been overthrown. On 4 April the commissioners were to begin their task by seeing all those worth £50 or more. But Norfolk did report immediate difficulties and raised fears for the future. Although these commissioners had behaved well, he was afraid that there would be great problems in raising the money generally in the country. In Norwich the mayor and leading citizens, whom Norfolk had approached, offered plate instead of coin and warned of the harmful effects that the demand would have on the local textile industry. Norfolk refused to accept plate there and then but agreed to report the offer to Henry and Wolsey, which he did, reminding them of how Henry VII had once coined 'dandiprats', small sub-standard coins. Was Norfolk in any way encouraging refusals? Or was he rather doing the best he could to obtain the grant, soothing local worries, and searching for practical solutions? He also agreed to 'bee a meane' to the king and Wolsey that the citizens and gentry of Norwich and Norfolk should only be charged if the other cities and counties of the realm agreed to the grant. This earned Norfolk a rebuke from Wolsey — it was a great error to make the grant of Norwich conditional — but, as Norfolk explained, that was not what he had done. By lessening fears of injustice, he was relieving legitimate worries rather than encouraging reluctance to grant. Norfolk also deferred 'practising' with men worth less than £20 in order to arrange that this should take place on the same day as in Suffolk: no one would then be influenced by news of refusals by their neighbours. If Norfolk had indeed been anxious to foment resistance, then he might rather have gone ahead provocatively. It is hard to read his first letter without sensing his diligent and sensitive handling of what was a difficult task.[1]

His second letter, written on 4 April, shows few signs of anything but careful, determined preparation. He had consulted with the duke of Suffolk about the grant: those worth £20 and above would be 'practised' in the counties of Norfolk and Suffolk between 6 and 8 April, those from £20 downwards, between 10 and 12 April. Admittedly these dates were slightly later than that mentioned in Norfolk's first letter, but there is no reason to suppose that this delay was due to more than understandable administrative complexities. Both dukes fully expected to have accomplished their task and to be back with the king on 22 April for the following St George's Day ceremonies of the order of the garter.[2] On 10 April Norfolk's tone was still optimistic, despite some problems. He had had 'no smalle besines' to bring the king's commandment to good

effect: the commissioners had sent him 200 refusers but he had
so treated them that no one in the end had maintained his
refusal. There were not twenty in the whole county worth £20
and above who had not granted. He trusted that 'right fewe
shall saye nay' so that 'I see greate likelyhode that this graunt
shalbe moche more than the lone was'. Letters of thanks would
give much comfort and would encourage others to grant. In
Norwich all had granted except some who were absent; it was
true nonetheless that these grants had not been made 'without
sheding of many salt teares oonly for doubte howe to fynde
money to contente the kinges highnes'. Where Wolsey had
expressed some surprise at the valuations, Norfolk insisted that
they were correct and offered to pay any difference himself,
confident that there was none. He was still planning to return to
London to prepare for the invasion.[3] By 14 April Norfolk could
report that only Lynn, Yarmouth and those worth less than £20
in one small hundred remained to grant.[4] He had been vigorous
and successful as commissioner in early April.

The duke of Suffolk had also been active. He had discussed
the grant (and particularly the need to co-ordinate their
respective negotiations) with the duke of Norfolk at the
beginning of the month.[5] On 11 April he reported to Wolsey
that he had been riding out various grumbles and grudgings
(further suggested by his statement that *now* [my italics] the
people were conformable) and had secured grants throughout
Suffolk, except from Ipswich where he was about to go. The
county gentry had been very diligent and deserved great
thanks. Nothing here hints that he was stirring up trouble. His
desire to know what authority the collectors should have to levy
the money if anyone refused to pay what he had granted
showed a prudent concern for the second stage of the operation,
in which those who were agreeing to the demand would be
called upon to pay.[6]

No letters to or from the dukes of Norfolk and Suffolk survive
for the weeks between 14 April and 30 April. It would be
interesting to know just what was happening in East Anglia at
this time. It is possible that resistance was growing and that
Norfolk and Suffolk concealed it. But it is far more likely that
nothing happened. Most of the inhabitants had agreed to grant
by 14 April and the remaining towns and hundreds can be

assumed to have followed suit. Once that was done there was, until the time of payment arrived, nothing more to arrange. Norfolk and Suffolk were sufficiently confident to leave East Anglia and attend the king on St George's Day.[7] It may reasonably be guessed that they discussed the Amicable Grant with Henry and Wolsey at this time. It is tempting to speculate that they influenced the change in policy — the reduction in the rate demanded — made at this time, but what is clear is that by late April they returned quickly to their respective counties.

The duke of Norfolk went back to implement the revised demand, intending to ride to all parts of the county of Norfolk. By 30 April he had dealt with half the inhabitants of Norwich and hoped soon to finish there and move into the county. He was clearly seeking acquiescence in half the original grant, one-twelfth, instead of one-sixth. He had also — in response to rumours that Wolsey had replaced the original demand in London with a benevolence — tried out what would happen in Norwich if the leading citizens were allowed to grant what they would, only to find that produced barely one-sixth of the original grant, that is a mere one-thirty-sixth. Norfolk had also run into some technical difficulties over the commissions that the collectors should have. But all in all Norfolk remained buoyant. 'I haue this day taken soche ordre with all the commissioners that I am in noo doubte the kinges highnes and your grace shalbee contentid with the graunte of this shire', he assured Wolsey. In no way did Norfolk appear to be blaming Wolsey for the concessions he had made in London (although he and Suffolk were to express concern at the confusion of policy later). Nor can Norfolk be shown to be implementing an independent reduction of the demand: Henry's letters to the city of London and to the marquess of Dorset, and Wolsey's offers in London, all predate Norfolk's actions and suggest an agreed, if varied, policy.[8] And it seems that the duke succeeded in persuading 'all Norff' to grant the reduced demand.[9] What Suffolk was doing in these days is not known. Hall tells us that by 'gentle handling' he persuaded the 'riche Clothiers' of Suffolk 'to geue the sixt parte', but this presumably took place in early rather than in late April.[10] There is no evidence that Norfolk or Suffolk were fomenting rebellion or encouraging resistance. Any such view, moreover, must deal with the very similar difficulties that the earls of Essex and Oxford and Lord Fitzwalter, commissioners in Essex, were facing. After mustering commissioners at Chelmsford and accepting grants on 1 May, they then met 200–300 refusers at Stansted on 7 May. Are they too supposed to be concealing their stirring up of troubles? If not, that would rather point to the possibility of spontaneous refusals and the consequent exoneration of Norfolk and Suffolk from such charges.[11]

Trouble did break out in the south Suffolk clothing towns in and around Lavenham, Sudbury and Hadleigh (disturbances that will be fully assessed later). There is not a shred of evidence that the duke of Norfolk provoked them. He had small territorial interest in that area: just a house at Stoke-by-Nayland. Contrasting his influence there with that of the earls of Oxford and Essex and Lord Fitzwalter he wrote in 1528 from Stoke in his own hand that 'that litle poure that I may make . . . is not within xxiiii or xxx myles of this howse'. If he had wished to start a rebellion it would have been much more sensible for him to have done so in Norfolk or in eastern Suffolk around Framlingham.[12] Nor was the duke of Suffolk influential around Lavenham: his Suffolk manors were somewhat to the east.[13] If Hall is right, Suffolk may have sparked off troubles by his successful persuasion of the rich clothiers who then warned their workers that they would no longer be able to employ them, leading to large assemblies of angry men. The people railed openly against the duke of Suffolk (and other commissioners), Hall says, threatening him with death. When he took steps that constables should confiscate men's harness, rumours of troubles increased.[14] But what all this shows is that the duke of Suffolk was zealously, perhaps too zealously, enforcing the grant. He does seem to have persuaded 'a greate parte' of the county to agree to the reduced demand.[15] The resistance he encountered was directed against him as the king's commissioner whose demands were jeopardising local employment, not a rising instigated by him for his own political ends. It reflects not his strength but his weakness. Still perhaps too much of an upstart fully to take the place of the de la Poles, he was more probably insufficiently well endowed in lands in Suffolk, and too often distracted by military and courtly duties, to have achieved a local dominance in that county comparable to that which enabled the duke of Norfolk to secure grants without provoking any rebellion in Norfolk.[16] It makes much more sense in general to see the dukes as reacting to circumstances which they had not only not created (except, perhaps, inadvertently), but rather had tried hard to forestall.

Faced by a popular rising, Suffolk and Norfolk responded vigorously, treating it as a military emergency. According to Hall, Suffolk could raise but a small number of men and those that came would only serve conditionally: 'they would defende hym from all perilles, if he hurte not their neighbors, but against their neighbors they would not fight.' Griffith says much the same about Norfolk's men. This does not show that relations between the dukes and their men on the one hand and the insurgents on the other were good; it points rather to the appalling dilemmas of allegiance that rebellions could provoke. Nonetheless Suffolk's gentlemen 'did so muche that all the bridges wer broken . . . so that their assemble was somewhat letted'.[17] If the rebels were intending to go on to London to petition the king (as Henry feared on 9 May),[18] then Suffolk's action may indeed have been important in setting geographical limits to the extent of the troubles. Norfolk, on hearing of the disturbances, joined Suffolk:[19] by 8 May the dukes were meeting together daily to discuss tactics.[20] They were not especially worried by the troubles in Suffolk: they feared insurrections that might spring up elsewhere more than that which they faced (or so they wrote).[21] Nonetheless on 9 May they began to gather their forces from both counties together: by 11 May they had 4,000 men.[22] According to Ellis Griffith, Suffolk wished to attack and to destroy the rebels while Norfolk refused because of the reluctance of their men to attack their fellows[23] (a caution Norfolk was to show for similar reasons during the Pilgrimage of Grace). Hasty punishment would, he wrote on 8 May, be dangerous.[24] Suffolk evidently bowed to the judgment of the older and more experienced Norfolk: it was Norfolk who wrote parts of letters to the king in his own hand and who talked with the rebels.[25] It is impossible to determine the numbers of rebels with certainty: estimates (to be discussed later) varied from 4,000 downwards.[26] The dukes sent John Spring, son of the great clothier Thomas Spring, and his brother-in-law Thomas Jermyn to the rebels 'to theim as of theim selfes to enduce theim' to submit.[27]

By 11 May the troubles were over: the dukes then felt secure enough to send home all but a thousand of their men.[28] Only the chroniclers tell us how the dukes brought the troubles to an end. According to Griffith, a deputation from the commons came to the dukes and, after a long conference, the dukes agreed to hear the people's grievances. A large number then came, all speaking at once. The dukes told them to go away and decide whether they would maintain their rebellion or submit. The dukes made it quite plain that the commons' action was against the king, council and the laws of the realm. If the rebels decided to submit, they should appoint one of their number to plead their cause. Sixty went to the dukes, who listened civilly to them. They then reported back to the body of the rebels. But after a series of divisions and misunderstandings among the rebels, sixty of them submitted to Norfolk, their leader explained their poverty 'and everything was smoothed among the people in that part of the kingdom'.[29] According to Hall, Norfolk sent to the commons to know their intent; and then went to them and heard their complaints. They agreed to depart; and then many came to Bures in their shirts and with halters about their necks to submit.[30] A letter by Norfolk and Suffolk describes the rebels' submission. On 11 May the dukes met a goodly number of people two miles on the Lavenham side of Bures: the inhabitants of Lavenham and Brent Eleigh 'cam all in theire shirttes, and kneling before us with pitious crying for mercy, shewed that they were the kinges moste humble and faithefull subgiettes and so wold contynue during theire lyves'. The dukes were going on to meet similarly penitent rebels from Sudbury.[31] Norfolk and Suffolk had dealt swiftly and tactfully with the rebellion. Hall wrote how the dukes 'so wisely handeled themselfes, that the commons wer appeised'.[32] Henry fully trusted them for he told the earl of Essex, when authorising him to raise men on 9 May, to take instructions from the dukes.[33] Wolsey thanked them for their 'wyse discrete and politique' behaviour in repressing the rebellious people of Lavenham and reducing them to the king's obedience, 'wherin ye haue deseruyd hygh and gret prayse with the kyng'.[34]

But did Wolsey later, and should we now, suspect Norfolk and Suffolk of showing too much leniency and sympathy towards the rebels, of reporting the possibility of a general insurrection with secret satisfaction, of using the disturbances as an argument to reduce Wolsey's influence with the king?[35] It is quite likely that the dukes sympathised with the plight of the commons. They wrote of 'this vnhappy people that this folisshely hathe vsed themselffs'. Hall noted that Norfolk was 'sory to heare their complaint, and well he knewe that it was true'.[36] But Norfolk and Suffolk conceded nothing. What they offered to do, according to the chroniclers, was to help the rebels obtain a pardon for the offences they had committed in rising, no more. And acceptance of a pardon implied an admission of guilt.[37] The commons 'found [the dukes] ready to listen civilly to their plaints, and to become their keepers and protectors against the king's ire for breaking the law'.[38] Norfolk pledged 'on my honor I will send to the kyng and make humble intercession for your pardon, which I trust to obtein'.[39] Norfolk and Suffolk themselves described how they 'tryed out iiii of the pryncipall of the offenders and caused the offenders selfes to take theim and present theim to vs moste humbly besechyng vs to bee meanes to the kinges highnes for theire pardon': after giving them sharp and sore lessons, the dukes promised to be suitors to the king for their pardon.[40] It would be rash to read into these promises any concessions on the grant. The dukes imposed on the rebels a particularly humiliating public parade of submission. Hall and Griffith say that the ringleaders (Griffith states fourteen) were sent or brought to London and imprisoned in the Fleet.[41] In their letter of 11 May the dukes wrote that they had kept four of the principal offenders from the assembly near Bures for further handling.[42]

Did Wolsey expect severer measures to be taken? In his letter thanking the dukes, already quoted above, Wolsey went on to urge them to set a fearful example to others. Since the offenders did not submit until armed force had been raised against them, they should now be more sharply punished than if they had submitted earlier.[43] It would be wrong to contrast this with Norfolk's and Suffolk's earlier suggestion to the king, while the rebels were still up in Suffolk, that if insurrections broke out in other shires, he should use 'some dulce meanes' because it might be dangerous to give out hasty punishment. That recommendation was made while the rebellion was still in being. It was merely tactical. 'Quod deffertur non aufertur', Norfolk wrote in his own hand (advice strikingly similar to his advice to Henry during the Pilgrimage of Grace).[44] On 11 May Norfolk and Suffolk wrote that they were intending 'to pacifye this matire according to the wordes of our Instrucions without sitting vpon any sessions considering that the wordes of oure said Instrucions purportithe not that we shuld so doo vnles by no faire meanes the rebellion mought bee pacified'. As at this time the government was still proceeding with the financial demand, that might well have seemed the most sensible course of action. Did Norfolk and Suffolk expect that only the ringleaders would be dealt with, suffering a spell in the Fleet, and an audience before the king's council, after which they would be sent home, while the majority would not be indicted? But nothing that Norfolk and Suffolk did precluded the possibility that in due course larger numbers of rebels might be prosecuted. In their dealings with the rebels Norfolk and Suffolk were very firm. At their submission near Bures the dukes

made a long rehersall the beste we coulde to agravate theire heynous offence declaring the same to bee highe treason and laying the soreste we could to theire charge as well of theire evell demeanor againste the kinges highnes as of theire rayling wordes.[45]

They repeated this on 17 May: 'at all tymes of theire submission we ever declared to theim that they had offendid the kinges highnes in highe treason and never made the matire to bee of les offence'. In reply to Wolsey's letter of 15 May (which does not survive) written immediately after the abandonment of the Amicable Grant and dealing with wider prosecutions, Norfolk and Suffolk insisted that 'without doubte we never thought nor ment but at the leste they should be indited of ryott and vnlawfull assemble'. Where Wolsey thought it convenient for the king's honour that the offenders should be inquired into and their offences 'founde by verdight', and that in the opinion of the judges their offence was 'but ryott and vnlawfull assemble', Norfolk and Suffolk insisted that 'vndoubtedly we were never of other opinyon but so to doo'. What had been troubling them was that Wolsey's and the king's earlier letters had told them that judges would be sent down to sit on commissions of oyer et terminer, and asked them what might be laid against the rebels: Norfolk and Suffolk wanted to inform the king and Wolsey of their views orally rather than in writing. Nonetheless they would be present the next day when the rebels would be indicted.[46] A special sessions of the commission of the peace was indeed held by eight JPs (the two dukes, Sir Robert Curson, Sir Robert Drury, Sir Richard Wentworth, Sir Anthony Wingfield, Sir Philip Tilney, Sir John Heveningham, Humphrey Wingfield and Thomas Jermyn) at Lavenham on 18 May: some 525 men were indicted for riot and unlawful assembly.[47]

Little should be made, in this context, of Norfolk's and Suffolk's earlier suggestions, mentioned above, that the demands being made by the crown needed clarification. Nothing in their recommendations provides evidence that the dukes welcomed the troubles or were supporting the rebels. When on 11 May they pointed out that the inhabitants of Norfolk and of a great part of Suffolk had agreed to grant half the original demand and would feel aggrieved if other counties were allowed to pay no more than they would grant of their good will, they were showing impeccable good sense and working out how best to raise the money the king needed, warning of the dangers of inconsistent and unjust policies.[48] A day later (12 May) they reported further details of the confederacy and noted ominously, that 'dyvers other contreys lay herkenyng to here that and they did stirr to haue doon the same'. They now went on to ask that whatever Wolsey decided upon — either a continuation of the 'practice' of a moiety of the original grant from those who had yet to grant or a general request for a benevolence — he should not ask them to enforce it until they had spoken with the king and him 'to declare and shewe more of that we haue hard and seen than we can wryte'. They went on to say that 'assuredly all thinges well considered that we here and see we thinke we neuer sawe the tyme so nedefull for the kinges highnes to call his Counsaill vnto hym to debate and determyne what is beste to bee doon', and that they implored Wolsey 'not to send for the oon of vs without the other'. [49] Should this be read as evidence that they were using the troubles against Wolsey, seeking to take credit for repressing the rebellion and to come down to the king and

criticise his leading minister? But that exaggerates the strength
of their position. Suffolk, after all, might be open to complaints
that his handling of the grant had provoked troubles in an area
under his authority (though no such charge was made). More
plausibly the letter should be taken at face value. The rebellion
was over, but it had only just been dispersed. Further news was
arriving of disaffection in other counties. A demand — it was
not clear whether for a half of the original demand or for a
benevolence — was still in force. There was some uncertainty
about just how the offenders of Suffolk should be dealt with. A
few days later the dukes explained themselves further. 'We
thinking not possible for vs by wryting so playnely to haue
declared the circumstaunces of the fact of the offenders as by
mouthe. And also heryng dayly many reportes out of other
shires of the light determinacion of the people there', they
thought it very necessary to come to speak with the king and
Wolsey. The somewhat defensive tone of this letter of 17 May
suggests some displeasure on Wolsey's part, but that should
not cast doubt on Norfolk's and Suffolk's motives.[50] Possibly
despite the dukes' insistence that they would not leave until
they were sure there would be no new troubles, Wolsey was
anxious that they should stay in East Anglia until the offenders
had been indicted.[51] On the other hand, if it was their earlier
letters and reports of disturbances that finally swayed the king
and the cardinal to cancel the demand, then Wolsey's
presumed annoyance with the writers of bad news would be
understandable. But it is important to note that Wolsey was in
no sense giving the dukes any new grievances against him by
exploiting the troubles against them. He rather wanted the
rebels punished precisely because this would reassert the
dukes' local standing which he saw as linked with that of the
king. To deal firmly with the rebels would be (as the dukes
repeating the wording of Wolsey's letter wrote) 'convenyent for
the kinges honor and *oure estimacions*'.[52] Crown, minister and
nobles are here working together.

A great difficulty in seeing in these letters tensions between
Norfolk and Suffolk on the one hand and Wolsey on the other is
that other commissioners sent very similar reports to Wolsey
and to the king. Unless one postulates some grandiose
conspiracy, this strengthens the case for seeing all

commissioners, including Norfolk and Suffolk, as loyally doing their best in difficult circumstances. The earl of Essex and Lord Fitzwalter reported on 9 May that on 1 May they had dealt with the commissioners at Chelmsford but not with the laity because of a great fair. This shows not their reluctance but their recognition of practical problems. They then arranged to deal with divers hundreds of the county, 'and thereupon practysed with theym accordyng vnto our instruccyons and with moche difficulty and persuasyons brought the most parte to condiscend and graunt to the kynges pleasure'. Is this to be taken as evidence that they were stirring up troubles: surely it reflects rather their very real problems. On 7 and 8 May they had certain townships — about 200–300 men — before them at Stansted 'whiche in no wise we kuld induce to no goode conformyte as concernyng the graunt of any money' saying they could not pay the subsidy let alone a new charge. They blamed these refusals on the example of the assembly of a thousand people in the neighbouring parts of Suffolk, and on threats that were made against the inhabitants of Essex when they went to market in Sudbury. They thought 'ther woll of lyklywode aryse such insurreccyons as hathe ben of late in the partyes of Suffolke. For we in no wyse doo lyke the maner of the demeanour of the people'.[53] A day later the earl of Essex was authorised to raise men to deal with any disturbance.[54] Then Essex and Fitzwalter had met with the earl of Oxford at Hedingham. By going to the borders of Essex and Suffolk with their household servants and by having others in reserve if necessary they had, they claimed, stayed the country.[55] These reports should be accepted at face value rather than be used as evidence to suppose that Essex, Fitzwalter and Oxford were fomenting troubles. And if they are taken as a true account, then they would rather point to the more general possibility of spontaneous popular refusals and the consequent exoneration of Norfolk and Suffolk from suspicion. Difficulties appear to have been very similar in different counties: in Suffolk reluctance to grant flared up into a short-lived rebellion. The reaction of commissioners was much the same: unless one is to claim a vast confederacy, it is most plausible to conclude that they were all doing their hardest, more or less skilfully and effectively, to secure compliance with royal demands.

It is also necessary to ask just what relations between Norfolk and Suffolk on the one side and Wolsey on the other were like. In these months Norfolk and Wolsey co-operated over patronage. On 14 April Norfolk warmly thanked Wolsey for helping to make him the king's lieutenant for the projected invasion of France:

> how goode your gra[ce] hath ben to me in this matier to advaunce me to the honor off the ledyng off the seid armye for the whiche yor graces fauorable and kynde remembraunce most humble and hertly I thanke the same and thogh I shall not be able in any part to recompence yor grace yet ye may be asseured I shall obserue and kepe fermly my wordes spoken to yor grace in yor bed chamber at Mr Larkes house.

There is nothing here to suggest anything but a pleasant and a close working relationship.[56] On 4 April Norfolk began a letter to Wolsey giving details of how he would 'practise' the grant and reporting the dangers of French sail cruising off the coast by mentioning the imminent death of John, Lord Marney, and asking Wolsey's favour to secure the wardship of one of his daughters against other suitors, considering that the king had promised it him. 'Moste humbly I beseche youre grace', he wrote, 'to help by youre good meanes . . . whiche matire eftesones moste humbly I beseche yor grace to haue for me in youre good remembraunce'. On 28 April he returned to this (incidentally showing how well-informed he was) on hearing that Marney was 'drawyng the draughts off deth, and Mr Butts [the royal physician] determynde he shuld not lyve after 5 owrys'. Would, he asked, the king allow Lord Fitzwalter and him to seize Marney's two daughters? Perhaps Norfolk felt it disagreeable to have to address a royal minister so obsequiously, or perhaps he sincerely thought it would be a great favour if Wolsey took an active interest in such a matter, but in either case it is abundantly clear that Norfolk was fully confident of receiving Wolsey's assistance, and from the outcome it may be deduced that he did.[57] Wolsey also effectively pressed the question of losses sustained by Norfolk's ship, even if his primary purpose was diplomatic rather than personal.[58] There is no sign that Norfolk was out of favour at this time: in January 1525 the imperial ambassador wrote how powerful the cardinal and Norfolk were in the kingdom and how much confidence their master placed in them.[59]

Was Norfolk in any way unhappy about Wolsey's handling of him during the Scottish negotiations in 1524? Their letters suggest a good working relationship cemented by trust. Wolsey did occasionally criticise Norfolk's actions but to use such comments alone as evidence of his attitude towards Norfolk would be quite misleading. On 1 August Wolsey told Norfolk that as 'ye knowe right well' 'the practise sett forthe for the said diett [i.e. the discussions between the duke of Norfolk and the chancellor of Scotland] was never ment ne intended on this side for any communication of peax' but simply to 'erect' the king [i.e. to declare him of age] and to extinguish Albany's government.[60] On 9 August Wolsey informed Norfolk that he had read his letter of 4 August

conteignyng diverse matiers, whiche I assure you be somwhat to the Kinges and my mervaile, and specially that ye have not wel and ripely taken and understonden such devices communications and letters, as hath passed upon the present charge to you committed. For, wher ye say ye never thought the contrary vnto nowe, but that ye shuld haue had auctorite sent vnto you, the Lord Dacres, and others, to haue mete and treated of peax, if the King the Quene and Lordes of Scotland wold have desired the same; I doubt not but that of your great wisedome, ye can wel considre, though ye had never been present at the debating of your charge, as ye were sundry and many times and almost at al communications, had thereof, that it were ferre discrepant from the Kinges honour to have the treaty of peax with Scotland concluded in a diet upon the Borders by Lieutenauntes or commissyoners.

Norfolk, Wolsey was alleging, had failed to understand his instructions despite various letters, despite his attendance at discussions of his responsibilities (presumably in the council), despite the very dishonourable and unusual nature of what Norfolk was doing. And yet in the same letter Norfolk was still entrusted by Wolsey with quite detailed and discreet tasks of persuasions.[61] Wolsey's letter of 15 August was not unfriendly; on 19 August he praised Norfolk's 'greate wisdome'; on 2 September Norfolk was sent the king's 'herty thankes'; on 15 September his 'grete and herty thanks'.[62] Norfolk was given discretion to judge whether or not the earl of Angus was to be allowed to return into Scotland: 'having best experience of the matiers there, so do therin, as ye shal think and perceyve to be most beneficial' for the young king, a striking delegation of authority to Norfolk, eloquent testimony of the trust placed in him.[63] Further hearty thanks came from the king on 28 September and again, for his good, discreet and diligent acquittal in present affairs, on 15 October.[64] From 20 October Norfolk repeatedly asked Wolsey to act as mediator between him and the king to obtain a licence for him to leave the borders, so subsequent praise by Henry and Wolsey, anxious that Norfolk should remain, is perhaps not wholly trustworthy. But it is significant that they should have had sufficient regard for him to wish him to continue in service. They 'moche commende and allowe your discrete ordre' taken with the earl of Angus and Queen Margaret. Wolsey promised Norfolk that 'suche causes of yor owne, as by reason of your absence can not be done this terme, shal and may right well be performed the next terme, without any yor losse or prejudice, wherunto doubt ye not I wol have good regarde'.[65] Surely this should all together carry more weight than (say) Wolsey's criticism of Norfolk for detaining certain letters, for which action Norfolk asked Wolsey not to be discontented with him till he had heard his excuses: he was coming to the king and to Wolsey with a right good will.[66] There is nothing to suggest that either Norfolk or Wolsey was annoyed with the other (except perhaps occasionally but then only briefly) as a result of the Scottish negotiations, no sign that Norfolk harboured any grievance against the cardinal. He was clearly active in early 1525. Norfolk went to see de Praet in early January; was present when Wolsey summoned de Praet to give him news from Italy in early February; was there when Wolsey berated de Praet after the seizure of his letters; and took part in discussions just before and after the news of Pavia arrived.[67] If he was not consulted about the change of plan in April, from a royal invasion to an invasion led by himself, that was because he was busily 'practising' the Amicable Grant in Norfolk and there is nothing to suggest that he was anything but delighted by his new military responsibility. Certainly he had been fully involved in the making of diplomatic policy in the previous months.

What were Suffolk's relations with Wolsey at this time? Had they been soured by the campaign of 1523? Much later, when it was open season for attacks against Wolsey, it was insinuated *inter alia* that Wolsey had not helped Suffolk at Montdidier with the money that would have enabled him to take Paris.[68] But that is not borne out by contemporary evidence of the campaign. Wolsey did give his attention to Suffolk's financial needs, as we have seen.[69] It was not, moreover, lack of money for his troops that ended that campaign. Nor do the chroniclers Hall and Griffith allude to this. According to Griffith, however, Wolsey did use the débâcle to discredit Suffolk. Wolsey 'governed the King's dominions as he saw fit' and he made such slander between Suffolk and the king that Suffolk stayed in Calais till Epiphany (having arrived there three weeks before Christmas) and then waited there (according to Griffith), till the feast of St John (6 May) before he was allowed in the king's presence.[70] Hall gives a comparable account except that, crucially, he saw the quarrel not between Wolsey and Suffolk but rather between Henry and Suffolk. Suffolk, and other captains, learning of Henry's 'displeasure' were 'sore abashed' and wrote to their 'frendes' (presumably at court) that Bourbon was certainly known to have broken up his camp, that their soldiers were dying, that victual failed, that there would be desertions. These explanations 'somewhat appeased' Henry, yet once Suffolk got to Calais on 12 December he 'there abode long' till 'frendes' of the duke and his captains had 'sued to the kyng for their returne'.

And when it was graunted and that they were returned, the Duke and the capitaines came not to the kynges presence in a long season, to their great heauynes and displeasure: But at the last all thinges were taken in good part and they well received and in great loue, fauor, and familiaritie with the kyng.[71]

But these accounts suffer from the distortion of hindsight. Suffolk's handling of the campaign had not, after all, been so bad: in many ways he had been obliged to follow on the actions of others; if the campaign had in the end been a disastrous failure nonetheless there had been 'glimpses of brilliant success'; he had secured the safe sheltering of the king's ordnance at Valenciennes, and he remained at Calais not in disgrace but as an earnest of Henry's determination to carry on the campaign should his allies show any enthusiasm.[72] If Henry was briefly annoyed with him, more important was Suffolk's speedy restoration to royal favour. On 10 May 1524 Suffolk jousted with the king.[73] Perhaps Henry did resolve never to trust his army to a lieutenant again,[74] which could be seen as a sign of little confidence in Suffolk, but rather to lead his army in person in future: but in late August, when an invasion was being mooted, it was Suffolk who was talked of as commander.[75] Wolsey's part in all this, if any, must remain obscure. There is, however, scanty support for any view of Suffolk as critical of Wolsey in this period. In October 1524 Wolsey was evidently assisting Suffolk in a private suit; in negotiations with the French he was firm in seeking the payment of Suffolk's promised pension and in maintaining Suffolk's wife's retention of the French crown jewel in her possession.[76]

By selective quotation, by systematic disbelief in all the letters, it is possible to put together an argument that the dukes of Norfolk and Suffolk deliberately stirred up refusals and disturbances in East Anglia or, in a milder version, that they made use of what was occurring spontaneously in order to discredit Wolsey's influence with the king. But careful reading of the evidence and consideration of the background suggest rather that there was no hostility between the dukes and Wolsey, and that what their despatches show is a willingness to do the best they could to achieve a difficult task in difficult circumstances. Here is not some neo-feudal connivance in an insurrection popular only in form, nor a semi-treasonable exploitation of rebellion and resistance for factional ends, but rather a shining example of the service nobility of later medieval England at work, straining to secure acquiescence in a stiff royal demand, soothing reluctant contributors and dealing firmly with rebellion.

Notes

1 B.L. Cotton MS, Cleopatra F vi fos. 336–8 (Ellis, *Original Letters*, 3rd series, i. 376–81; *LP*, IV, 1235); B.L. Cotton MS, Cleopatra F vi fo. 323 (*LP*, IV, iii appendix 36).
2 PRO SP1/34/fo. 131 (*LP*, IV, i 1241).
3 B.L. Cotton MS, Cleopatra F vi fos. 323–323^v (*LP*, IV, appendix 36).
4 PRO SP1/34/fo. 149 (*LP*, IV, i 1265).

5 PRO SP1/34/fo. 131 (*LP*, IV, i 1241).

6 PRO SP1/34/fos. 143–4 (*LP*, IV, 1260).

7 J. Anstis, ed., *The Register of the most noble order of the garter* (2 vols., 1724), i. pp. 367–9; *Cal. S.P., Spanish, F.S.*, p. 438.

8 PRO SP1/34/fo. 164 (*LP*, IV, i 1295).

9 B.L. Cotton MS, Cleopatra F vi fo. 325; Ellis, *Original Letters,* 3rd series, ii. 5 (*LP*, IV, i 1323).

10 Hall, *Chronicle*, p. 699.

11 PRO SP1/34/fos. 192–3 (*LP,* IV, i 1321); B.L. Cotton MS, Vespasian F xiii fo. 85 (*LP*, IV, i 1235).

12 Details of the duke of Norfolk's estates and houses from Mr G. Hill; I am grateful to Dr D.N.J. MacCulloch for reminding me of Norfolk's comment in 1528: PRO SP1/47/fo. 211 (*LP,* IV ii 4192).

13 *Ex inf.* Mr S.J. Gunn.

14 Hall, *Chronicle*, pp. 699–700.

15 B.L. Cotton MS, Cleopatra F vi fo. 325; Ellis, *Original Letters,* 3rd series, ii. 5 (*LP*, IV, i 1323).

16 I am grateful to Mr S.J. Gunn and Mr T.B. Pugh for their assessments of the duke of Suffolk.

17 *Ibid.*, pp. 699–700; *HMC, Wales*, i. p. ii. For the suggestion that relations between the dukes of Norfolk and Suffolk and the insurgents were good, and for the general view that the dukes 'countenanced' the rebellious commons, see M.E. James, 'Obedience and dissent in Henrician England: the Lincolnshire rebellion 1536', *Past and Present,* xlviii (1970), p. 51 and n.280.

18 *Historical Manuscripts Commission, 3rd report, appendix*, p. 202; *HMC, Wales*, i. p. iv.

19 Hall, *Chronicle*, p. 700.

20 PRO SP1/34/fo. 190 (*LP*, IV, i 1319).

21 *Ibid.* It is hard to grasp how the dukes can be accused of inflating the danger of the crowd when they wrote that they had the situation completely in hand (Woods, 'Individuals in the rioting crowd', p. 17).

22 B.L. Cotton MS, Cleopatra F vi fo. 325; Ellis, *Original Letters,* 3rd series, ii. 3 (*LP*, IV, i 1323).

23 *HMC, Wales*, i. p. ii.

24 PRO SP1/34/fo. 174^v (*LP*, IV i 1319).

25 E.g. PRO SP1/34/fo. 174^v (*LP*, IV i 1319) and *ex inf.* Mr S.J. Gunn.

26 See below, p. 136.

27 PRO SP1/34/fo. 209 (*LP*, IV, i 1343); Hall, *Chronicle*, p. 700: 'in especiall one Master Jermyn toke muche pain in ridyng and goyng betwene the Lordes and commons'.

28 B.L. Cotton MS, Cleopatra F vi fo. 325 (Ellis, *Original Letters,* 3rd series, ii. 5; *LP*, IV, i 1323); B.L. Cotton MS, Vespasian F xiii fo. 85 (*LP*, IV, i 1325).

29 *HMC, Wales*, i. pp. iii–iv.

30 Hall, *Chronicle*, p. 700.

31 B.L. Cotton MS, Cleopatra F vi fos. 325–325^v (Ellis, *Original Letters,* 3rd series, ii. 3–5; *LP*, IV, i 1323).

32 Hall, *Chronicle*, p. 700.

33 *Historical Manuscripts Commission, 3rd report, appendix,* p. 202.

34 B.L. Cotton MS, Appendix L fo. 12 (*LP,* IV, i 1324). 'Had not the Dukes of Norfolke and Suffolke appeased the people, the Cardinall had sung no more Masse' (W. Raleigh, *The Prerogative of parliaments in England* [Midelburge, 1628], p. 52. I owe this reference to Mr H. James).

35 E.g. D.M. Loades, *Politics and the Nation* (1974), p. 144; see also James, 'Obedience and dissent', p. 51 n.280; Woods, 'Individuals in the rioting crowd', p. 21 (Norfolk and Suffolk 'attempted to play "the good lords" . . . intervened directly with the government on behalf of the populace . . .').

36 B.L. Cotton MS, Cleopatra F vi fo. 325^v (Ellis, *Original Letters,* 3rd series, ii. 5; *LP,* IV, i 1323); Hall, *Chronicle,* p. 700.

37 I owe this point to my former undergraduate Miss Alison Williams.

38 *HMC, Wales,* i. p. iii.

39 Hall, *Chronicle,* p. 700.

40 B.L. Cotton MS, Cleopatra F vi fo. 325 (Ellis, *Original Letters,* 3rd series, ii. 4; *LP,* IV, i 1323).

41 Hall, *Chronicle,* p. 700; *HMC, Wales,* i. pp. iv–v.

42 B.L. Cotton MS, Cleopatra F vi fo. 325 (Ellis, *Original Letters,* 3rd series, ii. 4; *LP,* IV, i 1323).

43 B.L. Cotton MS, appendix L fo. 12 (*LP,* IV, i 1324).

44 PRO SP1/34/fo. 190 (*LP,* IV, 1319). For the contrast see James, 'Obedience and dissent', p. 51.

45 B.L. Cotton MS, Cleopatra F vi fos. 325–325^v (Ellis, *Original Letters,* 3rd series, ii. 4–5; *LP,* IV, i 1323).

46 PRO SP1/34/fo. 209 (*LP,* IV, i 1343).

47 PRO KB 29/157 mm. 5–6 (Controlment Roll) KB 9/497/ mm. 6–9, (on 18 May) (Ancient Indictments) cited by Woods, 'Individuals in the rioting crowd', pp. 1–24. For further discussion, and acknowledgments, see below pp. 136–40, 148 n. 5,14.

48 B.L. Cotton MS, Cleopatra F vi fo. 326^v (Ellis, *Original Letters,* 3rd series, ii. 5–6; *LP,* IV, i 1323).

49 PRO SP1/34/fo. 196 (*LP,* IV, i 1329).

50 PRO SP1/34/fo. 209 (*LP,* IV, i 1343).

51 PRO SP1/34/fos. 196, 209 (*LP,* IV, i 1329, 1343).

52 PRO SP1/34/fo. 209. (The crucial wording — my italics — is not in *LP,* IV, i 1343, as Mr S.J. Gunn has also noticed: I am grateful to him for discussions of this point.)

53 PRO SP1/34/fo. 192 (*LP,* IV, i 1321 is incomplete: the first quotation is omitted).

54 *Historical Manuscripts Commission, 3rd report, appendix, Marquess of Bath,* p. 302.

55 B.L. Cotton MS, Vespasian F xiii fo. 85 (*LP,* IV, i 1325).

56 PRO SP1/34/fo. 149 (*LP,* IV, i 1265).

57 PRO SP1/34/fo. 131 (*LP,* IV, i 1241); *LP,* IV, i 1292, 1073, 1936, 2203; ii 3324.

58 *Cal. S.P., Spanish, F.S.,* pp. 432, 438.

59 *Ibid.*, p. 432.
60 *State Papers*, iv. no. xlix p. 86 (*LP*, IV, i 549).
61 *State Papers*, iv. no. lii pp. 96–104 esp. pp. 100–3 (*LP*, IV, i 571).
62 *State Papers*, iv. no. liii pp. 104–8 (*LP*, IV, i 576); iv. no. liv pp. 108–10 (*LP*, IV, i 582); iv. no. lviii pp. 120–6 (*LP*, IV, i 615); iv. no. lxiii pp. 138–9 (*LP*, IV, i 662).
63 *State Papers*, iv. no. lxv pp. 149–52 (*LP*, IV, i 687).
64 *State Papers*, iv. no. lxvi p. 153 (*LP*, IV, i 701); iv. no. lxxiii pp. 174–82 (*LP*, IV, i 733).
65 *State Papers*, iv. no. lxxxiv pp. 218–23 (*LP*, IV, i 803).
66 *State Papers*, iv. no. cii pp. 271–2 (*LP*, IV, i 906).
67 *Cal. S.P., Spanish*, iii (i) no. 1 pp. 4–5; *State Papers*, vi. no. cix pp. 390, 394 (*LP*, IV, i 1083).
68 *LP*, IV, iii 6011.
69 See above, pp. 53–4.
70 Griffith, p. 11.
71 Hall, *Chronicle*, p. 674.
72 *LP*, IV, i 250 and comments from Mr S.J. Gunn.
73 Hall, *Chronicle*, p. 674.
74 *Cal. S.P., Spanish, F.S.*, p. 365.
75 *Ibid.*, p. 377; *LP*, IV, i 841, 619–20.
76 *LP*, IV, i 182, 736, 1093.

4 Archbishop Warham of Canterbury and the Amicable Grant

What was the attitude of Archbishop Warham of Canterbury to the Amicable Grant? Did he have no great love for Wolsey as a result of past humiliations? Was he at this time particularly annoyed by Wolsey's dissolution of some smaller monasteries?[1] Did he feel that he had been placed in an invidious position as chief commissioner of the Amicable Grant in Kent? Did he do less than he might to further the demand, did he stimulate or encourage opposition, was he secretly delighted at the refusals he was reporting? Or is it nearer the truth to suggest that, like the dukes of Norfolk and Suffolk, Warham was energetically and skilfully dealing with an impossible responsibility?

Archbishop Warham had assembled those chosen to be commissioners in Kent by 30 March. After he had 'practised' with them, some were willing to make a grant while others showed great untowardness. It required 'long communications and the best perswasions that we thowght most meytt' before they acquiesced: 'they all held themselues contented — or at the leste, noone of theyme said nay therunto' when the bill of names and sums expected was read out. Greater difficulties were to be feared, Warham thought, when the time came to collect the money which had just been agreed to. The commissioners complained of their poverty: they would need to sell lands and goods (itself not easy) if the grant were to be met. Some commissioners pointed to likely problems in practising with the people: if they met with refusals they intended 'not to wade verey far to persuade thayme, but to remytt the hole

96

Hundreds to me'. Warham himself was worried about refusals. He did not wish to have to send a multitude to the king, as his instructions said he should do. He also reported various rumours that were current: curses against the continual demands, cryptic attacks against Wolsey, complaints that the loan of 1522 had not been repaid, criticisms of royal policy in France past and present, maligning of Warham himself.

How far does this letter reveal Warham's own opinions? How far is he sympathising with and encouraging resistance? Nothing he wrote can have given any comfort to refusers. He had succeeded in getting the commissioners to grant. He had dealt with them quite severely. He had put his authority at risk — he had been told, to his face, he said, that by meddling and persuading in this matter he would lose the favour of the whole country. Only if Warham's letter is wholly dismissed as a pack of lies can any of this count against him. In writing to Wolsey he did not express an opinion about the Amicable Grant, except to question its size and timing. This practising 'for soe great sommes' might have been spared till the hot weather was over, till 'the cockowe tyme'. That sounds a reasonable comment from a man facing mitigated enthusiasm. Warham also reported criticisms of royal foreign policy and veiled attacks on Wolsey. It would be presumptuous to read these as expressions of Warham's own views.[2]

From Warham's letter of 15 April it is clear that he had set the commissioners to work. They in turn had sent to him those persons who denied the grant. Warham, if his account is trustworthy, lectured them very firmly. He accused them of conspiring among themselves which could cost them their lives, warned them of the king's wrath, pointed out the high costs of going before the royal council and threatened them with the loss of his own favour. His one apparent concession, that if the king did not cross over to France the money would be repaid, not only failed to convince (as the loan of 1522 had not been returned) but was a similar promise to that made by Wolsey in London, and not, therefore, proof of any independently subversive action by Warham. He refused to accept, from men who claimed that they were impoverished, offers of less than what was demanded from them. He added that if it later turned out that they were lying and were able to pay, their untruth

would cost them their goods. This was a threat, not a
concession.

Should Warham's self-portrayal be believed? His account
was addressed to Sir Thomas Boleyn and Sir Henry Guildford,
treasurer and comptroller respectively of the royal household,
who were about to assist him in Kent. No doubt it would be
useful for men so close to the king to be told how vigorously he
was pursuing his duty. But two features of this letter suggest
that it should be accepted. First, Warham went on to admit
that there was indeed much poverty and little coin — 'or els
theis men be too vntrewe'. Clearly he sympathised with the
pleas of the refusers. But, secondly, this did not influence his
attitude to his task of securing the demand. His main concern in
the second part of the letter was how to get the sums required,
and how to avoid, and if necessary deal with, any refusals and
opposition. The commissioners were to inquire into con-
venticles and assemblies and some of the ringleaders of the
refusers were to be sent up to be induced by the king and his
council which would have a salutary effect on other demurrers.
He himself was ready to see 'a great multitude' of refusers the
following week. Greater business was to be feared when the
time came to pay. It would be perverse to read this as an
encouragement of resistance. Warham's opinion that it would
not be profitable to examine those worth £20 downwards until
those then being practised had been persuaded was eminently
sensible. What is abundantly clear is that there were serious
difficulties in getting agreement to the grant in Kent and that
Warham, while sympathetic to pleas of poverty, was doing his
best to win over the recalcitrant.[3]

On the same day he warned Wolsey that should any of the
laymen sent up to the council be well treated, it would
encourage those at home to continue their resistance.[4] On 19
April he received further instructions and royal letters. He had
already been sending out his own letters to arrange a meeting of
commissioners at Canterbury on 2 May. He asserted his own
determination to press ahead with the demand: 'I have and
woll followe and execute with all my trewe and faithfull intente
dexteritie and diligence and refuse no cost peyne or perile to
accomplisshe the kinges graces pleasure in that behalfe as far as
I may possible'. Should this be read as disguising the opposite

of what it says, or should it, more plausibly, be taken at face value? He said he was handling the people 'with smothe wordes and rough' but they were furious and lewd. He foresaw great difficulty in getting the required sums but advised patience and could see some reasonable willingness to assist the king. Evidently Wolsey had been horrified by Warham's reports of what was being said against him. Warham promised to try to repress such tales and tried to soothe Wolsey's feelings. It was always the lot of counsellors to be maligned. Warham said that he too was abused. Behind his back he was called an old fool because he had been the first to grant and had thus caused these incoveniences. Some malicious persons said that it would be better for an old fool like him to take his beads in his hand than to meddle in temporal business pertaining to war. Warham added, in a breathtaking analogy, that just as Christ had been called by the Jews a seducer, traitor and worker by the devil, and had borne it patiently, every lewd word and deed, so would he. It seems unlikely that Warham would invent such stories: it is hard to see that they show him in a favourable light, except in so far as they demonstrate his nobility of purpose in carrying on the demand in the face of personal abuse.[5]

Eighty commissioners met at Canterbury on 2–3 May and reported serious difficulties. Inhabitants worth £20 upwards from various hundreds had come. They claimed that they had refused earlier because they feared that the king would have been more angry with them if they had then agreed to grant but later been unable to pay. They hoped that the king would not be displeased with them, and they offered their lives, bodies and goods to serve him. Significantly, Warham, Boleyn, Guildford and Cobham, whose three letters are our sources for this, added that 'this ther offertures and aunswers proceded only of theymselues and not by enducyng of us or any other yor graces commissioners'. Does this indicate the opposite, that the commissioners had told them to refuse, or to maintain their refusal, but at the same time to offer vague grants? Or should these proposals be treated more positively, as a sign of willingness to grant, but at a lower rate than had at first been requested? Possibly the inhabitants had got wind of concessions that Henry and Wolsey had already made elsewhere: the news that Henry had remitted the grant in

London had done no good in Kent, the commissioners reported. Moreover if this is evidence that they were stirring or encouraging refusals, it would implicate not just Warham but Boleyn, Cobham and Guildford as well, which is unlikely. There is no significant difference between their two letters to Henry and that to Wolsey; there is no hint of any criticism of the cardinal in the letters to the king. The chief commissioners did endorse the inhabitants' claims of poverty, but on the whole their letters suggest that there was a greater willingness to grant on which they no doubt hoped that it would be possible to build. They had promised to inform the king of their overtures — but refused to accept them there and then — and allowed them to depart till they heard further from the king. To Wolsey they recommended that it would be best not to summon those worth £20 downwards: they would be likely to cause much trouble for little profit and would grudge the cost of coming to Canterbury. That was good advice in the circumstances. All in all, it is difficult to conclude that Warham and the other leading commissioners were doing anything but their best.[6]

Warham's obvious delight at the news he had received by 8 May that the king had decided to reduce the sum demanded from the laity by half in no way shows that he had been lax in enforcing the earlier request.[7] On 12 May he pointed to continuing problems. There was 'an indiscrete and inordinate multitude . . . which at euery light fleeyng tale be inclined and kendled to il imaginations inuentions and ill attemptates rather than to good'. He agreed with Wolsey's advice of practising with small groups of the better sort but feared that it would now be hard to persuade them. The multitude persecuted all who complied: some honest and substantial men who had granted were thinking of leaving the realm for a season 'for fere of ill disposed people'. Warham warned of injustice if those who had granted were made to pay while those who had refused were allowed to get away with it. The commissioners were 'in greate grudge of the people'; their own 'light granting' was seen as the occasion of the troubles; if they had insisted on the poverty of the people, the king, they claimed, would not have enforced this matter. But if Warham emphasised his problems nonetheless he continued to take what steps he could and give advice to further the demand: he had made arrangements to keep watch on unlawful assemblies, and he thought it would be good if substantial men now attending Westminster Hall were sent back to their countries. In Warham's dealings with the laity of Kent, then, there is no evidence that he encouraged refusals, no sign that he attempted to use refusals against Wolsey, and if he sympathised with pleas of poverty, he nonetheless pressed on and never used poverty as a reason to give up altogether.[8]

Unfortunately there is little evidence for events in Kent by which to test Warham's letters. A brief account in Hall's *Chronicle* does, however, confirm Warham's account of difficulties. Lord Cobham, one of the chief commissioners, whom we have met above as a joint signatory of letters sent from Kent to Henry and Wolsey on 2–3 May, handled men roughly. He sent one John Skudder, who answered him 'clubbishly' to the Tower, an action that provoked popular grudging against him. Skudder was berated before the Lords in star chamber on 29 May. The people also 'euill entreated' Sir Thomas Boleyn at Maidstone. It is clear from Hall's details that Warham neither invented nor exaggerated the opposition he faced.[9]

But was Warham guilty of treating the clergy of Kent more lightly? Might he be suspected of partiality or leniency here? In response to orders to 'practise' an amicable and loving grant from the spiritual persons and clergy of the diocese of Canterbury,[10] he reported on 12 April that he had called together clergy from a large part of his area of authority, read them the preamble from the royal instructions but, 'after all other exhortations that I could devise and speke vnto thaym, I found but small towardnes'. He decided to summon them again on 20 April rather than urge them to grant immediately, since they had Easter duties that required them to serve in their cures and so that their refusals should not serve as an example to others. His chancellor had been elsewhere in Kent to practise with the clergy. Warham had also raised the grant with most of the heads of religious houses in Kent. They pleaded poverty and asked for time to consult with annexed convents and so on. Warham agreed to a delay 'advising thayme to loke more depely and more substancially on the matier and to make a better aunswer in avoiding of farther daunger'. He went on to tell Wolsey that monks in the houses that were being newly suppressed 'grudged sore therat' and suggested that it might be prudent to delay these dissolutions until after the Amicable Grant had been collected. Should Warham be criticised for agreeing to postpone demands from the clergy and the monks? Or, rather, was he sensibly preparing the ground for successful prosecution of the grant?[11]

There is nothing to show that Warham was taking any pleasure in the continuing disaffection among the clergy which he reported in his letter of 15 April. To report is not to condone. 'Credible persons' whom he had secretly sent to spy on the clergy had noted 'moche vntowardnes' among them. The clergy greatly begrudged the demand for a third of their goods at a time when they were about to pay an instalment of an earlier subsidy. If they agreed to grant they would live 'in contynuall pouertie'. If the king were to demand grants from them whenever it pleased him, that would be the destruction of the church and the end of hospitality: clergy would have to send their mothers and fathers begging. If they had money, or knew where they could get it, they would gladly contribute. If the king knew how poor they were, he would not demand so much. Laymen were refusing: the clergy would be the more blamed if they did not defend the goods of the church. Warham reported these grudges neutrally, adding 'if they be trewe, . . . ther is a great vntowardnes in the clergy for the whiche I am right sorey'. He would test them when he next saw the clergy. Meanwhile he asked for Wolsey's advice and 'that knowen I will helpe to the best of my power . . . to enduce the clergye to avaunce according to the kinges graces instructions'. Significantly — in view of clerical reactions to lay refusals — Warham recommended that any layman sent to Wolsey or to the king should be treated with exemplary firmness.[12] It is probably to this letter that Wolsey sent a reply that reached Warham on 17 April; on 21 April Warham again wrote of his difficulties with the clergy. What is striking here is that it was on Wolsey's recommendation that he had postponed the assembly of the clergy due to be held on 20 April until he had heard further Wolsey's 'most politike aduise how best to induce them' which Warham promised to follow. As this deferral was sanctioned directly by Wolsey, it should not be seen as evidence of Warham's indulgence of the clergy.[13]

Presumably no assembly of the clergy took place before news arrived that the king had reduced his demand from one-third to one-sixth of their revenues. Warham's subsequent request for confirmation that his own contribution should also be halved should not be seen as anything more than a cautious man's desire to have everything down in black and white. It must not be drawn out of context to support any notion that Warham had been opposing the grant earlier. Here it is more important to emphasise that far from suspecting any manoeuvres by Warham against him, Wolsey actually asked Warham's opinion of how the demand might proceed. Warham said it would be hard for him to show it — because, it may be assumed, it would be pessimistic — unless he could see some willingness in the clergy to make the grant. Unfortunately from his recent conversations with religious persons who had just received royal letters for the grant he had deduced 'more untowardnes than towardenes' both from them and from the secular clergy, especially from the religious. He would 'vse al meanes possible after my pouer wytte' to get them to 'inclyne' but these monks had sold their plate and jewels, sold or mortgaged their lands, and alleged marvellous great poverty.[14] Wolsey took Warham's advice and ordered him not to practise with the clergy until the outcome of the demands from the laity was known: Warham was very pleased.[15] It is quite clear that Wolsey had sought out Warham's advice and that he took it. This reinforces the view that the two men were here working together and that Warham was truthfully reporting genuine complaints and unwillingness to grant while doing his best to secure acquiescence in the demand.

A few weeks later, between 4 and 11 June, after the Amicable Grant was over, a riot took place at Bayham Abbey, on the border between Kent and Sussex, one of nineteen religious houses that were being dissolved. How far were the canons of Bayham among those religious men who, Warham tells us, begrudged the Amicable Grant? There are, unfortunately, no further details in his letters of who was complaining. How far was this riot the work of Warham? Was this his way of showing his annoyance with the Amicable Grant and with the dissolutions?[16] It is true that in mid-April he had recommended postponement of the dissolution while the grant was being practised, but that was to avoid upsetting too many interests at once and cannot safely be taken as showing Warham's opposition. There was later some local dissatisfaction at the dissolution of Tonbridge Priory but, judging from the tone of his letters, Warham was not especially sympathetic.[17] If Warham was supposedly expressing his opposition to the Amicable Grant, the timing of the troubles at Bayham is puzzling: the grant had by then been rescinded. Moreover it is far from clear that Warham had any ties with those accused of being ringleaders. Further, if the rioters were being spurred on from above, a more likely candidate would be George Neville, third Lord Abergavenny, much more influential than Warham on the Kent–Sussex borders.[18] Abergavenny had been suspected of complicity in the treasonable ambitions of the duke of Buckingham and had lost his posts in the Cinque Ports in 1521–2. In mid-May 1525 the dukes of Norfolk and Suffolk warned Henry to have 'a good regard' to Abergavenny if troubles broke out across the country. But there is no evidence that he encouraged refusals to the Amicable Grant and if he did nothing to quell the riots at Bayham there is nothing to suggest that he started them. Nor was he accused of anything: indeed on 22 June and 4 July he was recorded as present at the council.[19] More plausibly the resistance at Bayham was essentially a local defence of the abbey: no doubt the rioters hoped for support from Abergavenny and from Warham, as leading men in the region, but any attempt to link this with Warham's supposed opposition to the Amicable Grant would rest on the loosest of circumstantial evidence.

Moreover Warham was not the only senior churchman to report reluctance to grant. Bishop West of Ely wrote on 19 April of his difficulties and expressed sympathy with complaints of poverty: 'Sir oondowbtydly yt wold have made a man soroufull and heavie thowgh he had a right hard harte to heare the lamentacyon of the people'. He also asked how he should treat those who gave goods instead of money and warned of the dangers of insurrection if the levying of the money was not 'soberly and politiquely handeled'. There is no reason to suppose any special animosity between West and Wolsey; West's reports are similar to those of Warham; therefore Warham's letters should be accepted as sincere assessments of problems in Kent.[20] Bishop Longland of Lincoln wrote on 12 May that the clergy of Bedfordshire, Buckinghamshire and Huntingdonshire all claimed much poverty. Longland agreed with their complaints and suggested more widely spaced dates of payment. He was on his way to Spalding to meet heads of religious houses but — just like Warham in Kent the previous month — he refrained from calling the clergy until he had heard further from Wolsey.[21] The most telling evidence here is Thomas Benet's letter to Wolsey of 19 May. Benet had been ordered to induce the abbots, priors and clergy in the diocese of Salisbury to contribute to the grant but he had to report that none would consent to all of what was demanded. Many abbots offered part. None of the secular clergy, however, would give anything. In anxious tones, Benet asked Wolsey's advice, saying he had arranged to meet some of them in the week before Whitsun. The difficulties encountered by Benet are again similar to those faced by Warham. Yet Benet was Wolsey's chaplain and auditor: no one would suppose that he was in any way fomenting or encouraging troubles against his master. If Benet's problems were real and his reports of them credible, why should the same not be true of Warham's?[22] The conclusion must be that reluctance to grant and complaints of poverty were not prompted from above but were spontaneous. Perhaps opposition was especially strong and general among the clergy: Hall wrote that in every assembly priests said that they would pay nothing and that infamy was spoken in preachings.[23] In the light of such evidence, Warham, West, Longland and Benet are all most plausibly seen as servants of the crown doing their best, amid growing and real difficulties, to implement the royal will.

Further, it may be worth questioning just how far it was true that Warham and Wolsey disliked each other. From their letters written during the Amicable Grant, their relationship appears warm. Consoling Wolsey on the lewd words that the commons used about him, Warham said he would try to repress anything spoken against him, the dearest friend he had.[24] On 8 May Warham thanked Wolsey for his 'kynde lettres'.[25] On 12 May he concluded his letter with profuse thanks and pledges of service:

Finally in my most humble wise eftsones I thanke yor grace for yor singular goodenes afor mentionate both concernyng me and also the commons. . . . And if I may preceue or vndrestand any wey or meanes, howe to doo to yor grace any maner of acceptable pleasre or seruice in worde or dede, yor grace shalbe as suer of me to be redy to doo as the most assured frende or most diligent seruante that yor grace hath. And loth wold I be thus to write and subscribe with myne owne hand if it were not my true and feithful intent so to doo. Which my good mynde I beseche yor grace to accept in place and som parte of recompense of yor manifold goodenes shewed to me at al tymes.[26]

Of course there is a good deal of rhetoric here, but rhetoric should not be thought to be synonymous with hypocrisy. During the Amicable Grant, relations between Warham and Wolsey were good.

How bad had they been earlier? How far, even if they had been poor, did they remain so? It is likely that Warham had resented his replacement by Wolsey as Lord Chancellor in 1515[27] but that does not mean that he did not make the best of his reduced position later. It is possible that he attempted to challenge Wolsey's authority by inviting bishops to Lambeth in 1518–19 but it is uncertain just what this amounted to, and it was not repeated.[28] Warham was also involved in disputes with Wolsey over jurisdiction. It is important, however, to remember that 'frictions were inevitable in the pyramiding, appellate structure of the church legal system'. True, 'the cardinal's court was one of the most aggressive and powerful tribunals in the history of the English church to his time', but much of this aggression arose from the unusual position of Wolsey as legate.[29] Moreover what must be emphasised here is that it was not just Warham that felt the blast: all bishops did. In such circumstances Warham naturally defended his rights firmly, as did many other bishops, but that did not necessarily mean that personal relations between him and Wolsey were also affected. Warham's most vigorous protest against Wolsey's usurpation was formal and apologetic.[30] Their dispute over testamentary jurisdiction appears less important than has sometimes been suggested. In October 1523 Warham explained to Wolsey's registrar that he had only raised the matter because his friends had warned him that those who were not content with this agreement, who were many and of good authority, would have put Warham and his officers in danger of a *praemunire* suit. He added that the arrangement that had been reached would cost Wolsey nothing and would remove Warham from any such perils. Warham thought it quite satisfactory and hoped that it would be concluded without delay 'considering the great kindness that I find daily in my lord Cardinal's grace'. It would be presumptuous to infer irony here.[31] A composition between archbishop and cardinal was made in January 1523.[32] Was it humiliating for Warham? Did his letter of 12 January betray obsequious devotion? Or might Warham have been less than sincere in writing of Wolsey's 'tendre love', of 'how good and gratious I find you toward me'?[33] Perhaps some bishops opposed Wolsey, on other issues, in the convocation of 1523,[34] but there is no sign of any such action by Warham. In early 1525 he returned to the question of testamentary jurisdiction, but again presented it as a complaint made to him by others. He asked for it to be deferred till he would see Wolsey personally after Easter,[35] another indication of friendly relations between the two men. On 6 March Warham thanked Wolsey for taking his plain writing graciously and added that without Wolsey's undoubted favour he would not have attempted to disclose his mind so openly. He refused to believe any of the reports that were being circulated in order to create dissension between them. They would not cause him to mistrust Wolsey's goodness of which he had such solid proof that nothing could shake. He esteemed Wolsey's favour a hundred times incomparably more than the private cause of a testator's widow. He would defer proceedings in the current matter of John Roper's testament until he saw Wolsey after Easter. He trusted that Wolsey would not claim any right to proceed in testamentary causes.[36] To see a bitter running conflict here is to read far more into the evidence than is there. To conclude from this that the archbishop would then go so far as to foment, or to exploit, opposition to a royal demand to do down a royal servant to whom he professed affection and regard, despite disputes over jurisdiction, is to fly in the face of the evidence and to imply implausible levels of hypocrisy.

Notes

1 Cf. esp. J.J. Goring, 'The riot at Bayham Abbey, June 1525', *Sussex Archaeological Collections,* cxvi (1978), pp. 1–10; 'Warham displayed a stubborn lack of enthusiasm as commissioner in Kent for the grant and clearly sympathised with the clergy and laity he was appointed to assess'; M.J. Kelly, 'Canterbury jurisdiction and influence during the episcopate of William Warham 1503–1532', University of Cambridge Ph.D. thesis, 1965, p. 312; and many brief remarks.
2 B.L. Cotton MS, Cleopatra F vi. fos. 339–40 (Ellis, *Original Letters,* 3rd series, i. 369–75; *LP,* IV, i 1243).
3 B.L. Cotton MS, Cleopatra F vi. fos. 347—9 (Ellis, *Original Letters,* 3rd series, i. 359–67; *LP,* IV, i 1266).
4 B.L. Cotton MS, Titus B i fo. 274 (*LP,* IV, i 1267).
5 B.L. Cotton MS, Cleopatra F vi. fos. 350–350v (*LP,* IV, iii appendix 39).
6 PRO SP1/34/fos. 173–4, 185 (*LP,* IV, i 1306, 1311); B.L. Cotton MS, Vespasian F xiii fo. 133b (*LP,* IV, i 1305).
7 PRO SP1/234/fo. 240 (*LP,* appendix 457).
8 B.L. Cotton MS, Cleopatra F vi. fos. 341–341v (Ellis, *Original Letters,* 3rd series, ii. 8–12; *LP,* IV, i 1332.
9 Hall, *Chronicle,* pp. 699, 701–2.
10 B.L. Cotton MS, Cleopatra F vi. fo. 330 (*LP,* IV, iii appendix 34). For a suggestion that Warham 'took an active part in the clerical resistance to the loan', see Clark, *English provincial society,* p. 21.
11 PRO SP1/34/fo. 145 (*LP,* IV, i 1263).
12 B.L. Cotton MS, Titus B i fos. 273–4 (*LP,* IV, i 1267).
13 B.L. Cotton MS, Cleopatra F vi. fos. 350–350v (*LP,* IV, iii appendix 39).
14 PRO SP1/234/fo. 240 (*LP,* appendix 457). For a suggestion that Warham topped the long list of clerical defaulters, see Clark, *English provincial society,* p. 21.
15 B.L. Cotton MS, Cleopatra F vi. fo. 341 (Ellis, *Original Letters,* 3rd series, ii. 8; *LP,* IV, i 1332).
16 Goring, *loc. cit.,* p. 1.
17 PRO SP1/34/fo. 145 (*LP,* IV, i 1263); *LP,* IV, i 1470–1, 1459. *Pace* Clark, *English provincial society,* p. 22.
18 Goring, *loc. cit.,* p. 5.
19 Clark, *English provincial society,* offers no supporting evidence for his suggestion that Abergavenny may have encouraged resistance (p. 22).
20 B.L. Cotton MS, Titus B i fo. 271–272v (*LP,* IV, i 1272).
21 PRO SP1/34/fo. 198 (*LP,* IV, i 1330).
22 PRO SP1/34/fo. 211 (*LP,* IV, i 1345).
23 Hall, *Chronicle,* pp. 696, 701. There is no evidence of any clerical refusal or resistance in East Anglia.
24 B.L. Cotton MS, Cleopatra F vi. fo. 350 (*LP,* IV, iii appendix 39).
25 PRO SP1/234/fo. 240 (*LP,* appendix 457).
26 B.L. Cotton MS, Cleopatra F vi. fo. 341v (Ellis, *Original Letters,* 3rd series, ii. 11–12 (*LP,* IV, i 1332).

27 G.W. Bernard, *The power of the early Tudor nobility: a study of the fourth and fifth earls of Shrewsbury* (Brighton, 1985), pp. 21–2.

28 Kelly, thesis cit., pp. 160–3.

29 *Ibid.*, pp. 180–1.

30 Ellis, *Original Letters*, 3rd series, ii. 41–2.

31 *LP,* III, ii 2633 (contrast Kelly, thesis cit., p. 183).

32 *LP,* III, ii 2752.

33 Kelly, thesis cit., pp. 185, 187; *LP,* III, ii 2767.

34 D. Hay, ed., *The Anglica Historia of Polydore Vergil, Camden Society*, 3rd series, lxxiv (1950), p. 307, is the only evidence.

35 *LP,* IV, i 1118.

36 Ellis, *Original Letters*, 3rd series, ii. 43 (*LP,* IV, i 1157).

5   Poverty and the Amicable Grant

Everywhere in April-May 1525 there were cries of poverty. The same refrain was heard from the commissioners, from the parish clergy, from the textile workers of Suffolk. Of course anyone who was being called upon to make a grant to the king had an obvious motive for pleading poverty. But how far were such pleas, in the circumstances of spring 1525, sincere? Was the poverty of those being asked to contribute the reason for the failure of the Amicable Grant?

Complaints were certainly widespread. A good number of the commissioners whom Warham gathered at Otford on 30 March asserted that they could not make as much as they had for the last subsidy — far less than was now being demanded — without selling their lands and goods.[1] A London alderman told Wolsey that because 'diuerse merchantes be decaied by the seas, and suretiship, and other waies' since 1522, the valuation made that year could not be achieved. Hall also noted pitiful curses and weepings.[2] The clergy of Kent would live in 'contynuall pouertie' if they paid the grant: as it was, their houses were in decay and more demands would lead 'to the vtter vndoing and destruction of the same as they saith it is almost already and so hospitalitie shuld ceasse. . . . If ther shuld nowe be any newe contribution demaunded the Church shuld be vtterly destroyd'.[3] The clergy of Bedfordshire, Buckinghamshire and Huntingdonshire alleged much poverty. 'They cane haue noo money for ther cattall nor corn': they could not collect rents from their farmers.[4] Those inhabitants worth £20 upwards in Kent who were berated by Warham claimed that they were 'decayed': 'many alleging greate

110

pouerty and decaye in their goods', 'some in brennyng of their
barnes and other howses with stuff therin'; some had been
defrauded by 'shrewd' debtors.[5] Warham noted that some in
Kent (it is impossible to determine which group he meant)
were at their wits' end, 'rekonyng theymselues, theyr childrene
and wyfes, as desperates, and not greately caring what they
doo, or what become of thayme'.[6] The inhabitants of
Cambridgeshire and the Isle of Ely alleged 'great losses and
decayes'.[7] After the disturbances in Suffolk the rebels'
spokesman roundly declared to the duke of Norfolk: 'My
lorde . . . sithe you aske who is our captain, for soth his name is
Pouertie, for he and his cosyn Necessitie, hath brought vs to this
dooyng'.[8]

Should these pleas be accepted? One difficulty must be faced.
Dr G.L. Harriss has shown how late medieval theory held it
unthinkable for subjects to deny the crown support in time of
necessity. Necessity created an overriding obligation. Direct
refusal of financial assistance was therefore unusual. What was
more common was for 'the subject [to] affirm his desire to assist
the king but his inability to do so'.[9] Such claims were heard in
the early fourteenth century and were widespread in the
fifteenth. They were common during the Amicable Grant. In
early April Warham reported from Kent that men accepted
that the king might have as much as they could spare but
asserted that they were unable to contribute as much as was
required.[10] The refusers summoned before him on 15 April
protested that they had as good and as loving minds as any
subjects should have towards their prince, 'and if their goodes
wer according to their good willes, they wold neuer denye to
pay the demaund'.[11] If the clergy of Kent 'hadd money or knew
how to come by it, they wold right gladly contribute according
to the kinges graces demand'.[12] The Kent commissioners
reported to the king in early May how those who had appeared
before them declared that

if ther power and substaunce wer as good as ther willes they wold depart with
euery thing that yor grace wold demaund of theym, . . wisshing that they
hade now asmoch goodds as euer they had in ther lives and then yor grace
shuld right well perceve howe liberally they wold contribute to your grace.[13]

In Norwich the mayor and aldermen told the duke of Norfolk

that while it would be very commodious to invade France, they were unable to raise the money demanded.[14] The problem, then, is to assess these claims of poverty. Were they just stock responses in recurring constitutional-cum-political bargaining over royal financial demands or were they, in the circumstances of 1525, genuine statements of fact? Were men unwilling, or were they unable, to pay?

How much support was there for contemporary assertions of poverty? How far did the government and commissioners endorse them? On 15 April Warham, writing to Sir Thomas Boleyn and Sir Henry Guildford, admitted 'in good faith, I thinke ther is a great pouertie in Kent and lack of money as hath ben seen many yeres, or els theis men be too vntrewe'. 'I have been in this shire twentie yeres and above', he continued, 'and as yet I have not seen men but wold be conformable to reason, and wold be enduced to good ordre, tyll this tyme. And what shuld cause theym now to fall into this wilful and indiscrete wey I cannot tell, excepte pouertie and decaye of substaunce bee cause of it.'[15] Writing to Henry VIII on 3 May the chief commissioners in Kent firmly declared that 'here is greate pouertie'. Several men 'which lately haue been at diuerse fayres in this countey, wher men having much wares and catalles to be sold, haue in maner departed thens without any sale therof orels they must haue sold their ware more than half vnder the value, money is so scarce'. Rents were not being paid: 'diuerse landed men which shuld now abowght this season receive thair rentes can litell or nothing gete of thair fermors, alleging that they can gete no money for corne or cataile'.[16] Warham himself claimed that his half year's rents received from his farmers at Easter amounted to only £22, from the tone of his remarks obviously a derisory sum.[17] The commissioners did not think it worth practising with those worth £20 downwards because 'some of theym having skante money to bring theymselves to Canterbery or other places' would sore grudge the cost.[18] Bishop West of Ely reported pleas of poverty on 19 April. Many inhabitants alleged losses by fire and by murrain and made much dolour and lamentation. 'Sir oondowbtydly yt wold have made a man soroufull and heavie thowgh he had a right hard harte to heare the lamentacyon of people specyally in thies quarters not only of suche as bee poore men but allso of suche as heretofore were takyn for substauncyall and richemen'.[19] When Wolsey told the Londoners that it was better that some should 'suffre indigence' than that the king should lack, he was implicitly admitting that they were close to poverty.[20] According to Hall, the duke of Norfolk acknowledged the truth of the plight of the rebels in Suffolk. When their spokesman told him that their captain was poverty and that they feared unemployment, Norfolk was 'sory to heare their complaint, and well he knewe that it was true'.[21] None of Norfolk's letters directly support this, though perhaps his approval of the proposals by the mayor and aldermen of Norwich that plate should be accepted and dandiprats coined might be taken as suggestive.[22] According to Griffith, the Suffolk rebels' pleas of poverty were finally admitted. After Wolsey had lectured those who had been brought up to London and kept in the Fleet for a period, he ordered them to settle with the keeper of that gaol for their meat, drink and garnish. The weaver who had spoken for the rebels got on his knees and besought Wolsey 'to hear me unfold the poverty of our lives, inasmuch as we have not, God is my witness, or here, or in our country, fourteen shillings in money'. When they returned home they would have no means of providing for themselves or their families unless they were employed again, which they feared they would not be: 'for this reason we beseech your grace to look mercifully on our poverty'. After 'a long process', Wolsey said that the king would pay for their board and lodging in prison, and ordered the keeper of the prison to give them each four score pieces and ten of silver and to set them free.[23] What is legend and what is truth cannot easily be determined but there is no doubting the impression that Wolsey ultimately recognised their poverty. When the government reduced and then abandoned the Amicable Grant, such recognition was also put forward. From the marquess of Dorset's reports from Warwickshire and from Wolsey's from London, Henry saw (he told the Londoners) that

your powers and abilities be not equyvalent and correspondent vnto yor good myndes ne ye may commodiously performe the same [i.e. pay the demand] without your grete detryment and extreme hynderance & decay ... not willyng you in any wise to be so ouercharged in this benyvolent graunte as shulde be to yor extreme impouershing.

Henry was here acknowledging the fact of poverty.[24] So was Wolsey when he told the mayor and aldermen of London how it was his suit for them to the king, showing their 'great losses', the 'charges that you continually sustein', that had persuaded the king to reduce the demand.[25] When Henry finally cancelled the Amicable Grant he explained that 'some haue enformed me that my realme was neuer so riche, and that there should neuer trouble haue risen of that demaunde, and that men would pay at the first request, but now I finde all contrary'.[26]

The difficulty throughout is that all these references to poverty might be no more than moves in an elaborate game. People would say not that they did not want to pay but that they did wish to grant but were unfortunately too poor to do so. Governments would say not that the weight of opposition had compelled them to reduce or to abandon their demand but that they were mitigating or removing it because they now realised how poor the people were. It was a way to avoid treasonous resistance on the one hand, a way to save face on the other. But sometimes poverty might be genuine all the same. Governments could conceive of it as a proper reason for not demanding taxation. In 1521 Henry informed the earl of Surrey that it was not possible for the king 'in this harde and dere yere' to summon a parliament and secure a grant. 'For remembering the povertie of the people of every condicion, being decayed and in necessitie, by reason of this scarcitie, though they were benevolently mynded furthwith to graunte suche a subsidie to the Kinges Grace' it could not be levied for three years, at least, 'till suche tyme as God, of his goodenesse, by more fertile and plentuous yeres shall releve their indigence and povertie'.[27] Moreover the tone of the comments quoted above suggests that the situation in spring 1525 was serious. Several times hard-headed commissioners included in reports of their difficulties comments which show them as accepting complaints of impoverishment. Further, while most of the debate was indeed conducted within the framework of notions of necessity and obligation and of pleas of poverty, nevertheless there were some hints of outright refusal, itself a sign of attitudes approaching desperation. In London those who were consulted in the wards refused to grant a benevolence: 'the which they openly denied, saiyng that they had paied inough before, with many evill wordes'.[28] 'The burden was so greuous, that it was denied'.[29] 'In the same season through all the realme, this demaunde was vtterly denied, so that the Commissioners could bryng nothyng to passe'.[30] In mid-May Warham talked of 'almoste al the people obstinatly sett not to graunte'.[31] Might this not be indirect support for the pleas of poverty that were being advanced?

Many of these pleas emphasised shortage of coin as much as, or rather than, indigence, a complaint that would also be heard in 1536. Was there a general coin shortage? The mayor and aldermen of Norwich told the duke of Norfolk that they could not raise the money demanded of them but instead offered 'to make shift with all the plate they have': 'assuredly', commented Norfolk, 'none of theim had so moche reddy money as I desired of theim'. Norfolk suggested that this plate be accepted and 'dandiprats', small, substandard coins, be coined from it, as Henry VII had done, presumably in 1492. He added that 'those that haue most aduaunced this matire with me doo shewe vnto me that they believe that is skant somoche money within the shire as the Rates shall extende vnto'.[32] Bishop West of Ely wrote that the inhabitants of Cambridgeshire and the Isle of Ely complained that 'thei have no money to paye nor thei cold fynde no mean howe to get or make any money'. Even if they would sell their land and cattle for half their cost, no man in the country had money to buy. 'And to borowe any money the knew not wher ne of whome for thei sware ther was allmoste no money left in the cuntrey'.[33] In early May the Kent commissioners noted 'specially lacke of money'. Men having wares and cattle to sell had departed from fairs without selling anything; they could have secured sales only by selling for half their values. Farmers said they could get no money for their cattle and corn and so were unable to pay their rents. That prices were being so greatly driven down is further evidence of acute shortages of coin.[34] Warham's description of clergy and monks who 'haue solde their plate and iowelles and . . . haue layed their landes to morgage and some haue solde the landes of the churche' suggests shortages of ready cash.[35] More significant were the rumours that Warham had heard earlier:

'if suche as haue money wold lend vnto thayme that lakkith money, yet all the money in England besides that which is receivyd for the Kinges vse alredy, shall not be sufficient to performe the graunts of the Parliament not yet paide'. It would be the impoverishing of the realm and the enriching of France if the king were to have all this money and to spend it in France.[36] One George Cob saw the demand as 'a gret robyng of money howte of the contre'.[37] Bishop West asked what the collectors were to do if people who lacked money gave them stuff instead.[38]

There were clear signs of general monetary difficulties in the months before the Amicable Grant. Henry was displeased with the rulers of the Netherlands 'for enhaunsyng his coyne there, which was a cause that money was daily conueigned out of the Realme'.[39] Complaints that the rise in the exchange rates of English coins, especially the angel and the rose, was draining England of money were frequent in Wolsey's negotiations with the imperial ambassadors in late 1524 and early 1525.[40] In April 1525 Warham heard how some said that

so moche money is sent and spent out of this Realme already, with conveyaunce of English gold in to Flaunders by Englishe merchauntes to thaire singuler advauntage, by force wherof some say the Kings Grace must coyne copper and brasse for gold and silver, as spent and gone, which shuld be to the great reproche of this realme.[41]

There may well have been an unusual shortage of coin at the time the Amicable Grant was set under way. Possibly there was also a more general shortage of liquidity. Since the late 1480s there had been an increasing problem arising from the failure of governments to adjust the value of English coins in line with changes in the value of French and Netherlands coins. Because English coins, whose purity was renowned in northern Europe, were increasingly undervalued, that is worth more as bullion than their face value as coins, they were bought up and exported by speculators. Proclamations revaluing English gold and silver coins in 1522 proved insufficient; not until 1526 did the government firmly address the problem. But that the government acted at all strongly suggests that coin was indeed in short supply.[42] The 1523 subsidy act allowed payment to be made in foreign coins and in plate, specifying the price per ounce for each type of plate.[43] Before it was passed there was some discussion about the total coinage in circulation. A distinction was made between wealth on the one hand and quantity of coin on the other. The crown was demanding, in 1523, a tax of one-fifth. But

it was proved that there was not so much money, out of the kynges handes, in all the realme, for the fifth part of every mannes goodes, is not in money nor plate. For although fiue men wer well monyed, five thousand were not so, the gentleman of landes, hath not the fifth part of the value in coyne: The Merchaunt that is riche of Silke, Wolle, Tynne, Clothe, and such Merchaundise, hath not the fifth part in money, the husbande man is riche in corne and cattell, yet he lacketh of that same. Likewise viteilers and all other artificers, be riche in housholde stuffe, and not in money, and then consequently, if all the money wer brought to the kynges handes, then men must barter cloth for vitaile, and bread for chese, and so one thyng for another.

The sum demanded 'was impossible to be levied, and if all the coyne wer in the kynges handes, how should men liue?' Calculations were made then to show that there was £1m. in coin in the realm (a modern estimate is £1.67m).[44] If Wolsey was accurate in 1523 in claiming that a tax of 4s. in the £ would produce £800,000, then on that basis a demand for a sixth, as in 1525, would have produced £666,666. More plausibly, given that the loan of 1522–3 levied at the rate of one-tenth produced some £200,000, the Amicable Grant should then have produced £333,333. The acute strains on liquidity caused by such a demand are obvious, even if the figures are guesstimates. Those who complained of lack of coin in 1525 may well have been telling the truth.

These references to 1523 raise the question of earlier financial demands by the crown. Were these sufficiently great and burdensome to justify cries of poverty in 1525? Had men given so much to the crown in the years immediately preceding 1525 that they could now give no more? Crown financial demands in the years from 1522 to 1525 had certainly been enormous. Undoubtedly there was a vidid awareness of repeated royal demands. 'The people sore grudgethe and murmureth, and spekith cursidly emong theymselues as far as they dare; seying that they shall neuer haue rest of paymentes'.[45] The weaver of Lavenham said that the rebels wanted to go to the king 'to complain of the Cardinal on account of the taxes which he set men one day after another to demand of them'.[46] In Kent 'the people . . . began to accompt the loanes and subsedies graunted, so that thei rekened the kynges Tresure innumerable, for they accompted that the kyng had taken of this realme, twentie fiftenes, sithe the xiiii yere of his reigne'.[47] Londoners called upon for a benevolence in May said that 'they had paied inough before'.[48] Some of the Suffolk rebels preferred to die like men in their quarrel with those who were 'daily despoiling them of whatever God sent them for the labour of their hands'.[49] An instalment of the subsidy granted in 1523 was due by 9 February 1525 but was in fact in most cases still being paid at the time the Amicable Grant was being demanded. Dr R.S. Schofield's table shows that only 19% of what was due had been paid by 9 March: in many places then the subsidy was in men's minds just when new demands came.[50] The inhabitants of Essex assembled at Stansted on 7 May declared that 'they had not wherewith to pay the kynges subsidye. And to graunte to a ferder charge seyng they had not wherewith to pay thother they wolde in no wyse assent'.[51] Warham referred to the problems arising from current requests 'specially wher other grauntes of the Parliament bee nowe payable'.[52] It is worth noting by contrast how carefully the dates of payment of the various taxes of the 1510s had been staggered: the first fifteenth and tenth on 1 July 1512, the second on 2 February 1513; the poll tax on 1 July 1513; the next fifteenth and tenth at Easter 1514; the subsidies on 24 June 1514, 21 November 1515 and 15 October 1516, and the final fifteenth and tenth in November 1517.[53]

Men were also concerned by the non-repayment of the loan of 1522–3. That had been due to be repaid after the first instalment of the subsidy had been collected, which was done in early 1524, but it had not been. Hall says that in 1525 bills were set up in all parts of the realm, some saying 'the kyng had not paied that he borowed'.[54] 'Ther is a grudge newely nowe resuscitat and reviued in the myndes of the people', wrote Warham from Kent in early April, interestingly hinting at earlier discontents, 'for that the lone is not repayed to thayme vppon the first receipte of the graunte of Parliament, as it was promised thayme by the commissioners, shewing theym the

Kings Graces instructions conteynyng the same, signed with his Graces own hand'. The common voice was that if they were compelled to pay the Amicable Grant they would do so only provided the loan was counted part of it.[55] When Warham tried to lull suspicions that the king would keep the Amicable Grant even if he did not invade France, rather than repay it, as Warham promised, he was reminded that he and other commissioners had similarly promised that the loan would be repaid, which it had not been.[56]

The loan of 1522–3 was certainly astonishing. Commissioners were sent out to make fresh valuations which were used as the basis of a great loan.[57] The first part was a loan from the laity levied at the rate of 10% on those worth from £20 to £300, at the rate of 13⅓% on those worth between £300 and £1,000 and at the discretion of commissioners on those worth above £1,000. It was raised in late summer and early autumn 1522.[58] In spring 1523 a loan was levied at the rate of 10% on laymen worth between £5 and £20.[59] These loans produced £105,000 and £57,000 respectively, with a further £43,000 from the nobility, various laymen (presumably rich merchants), the city of London and the town of Calais. Moreover these sums were speedily paid: £100,000 of the £105,000 was paid by February 1523, £51,000 of the £57,000 by 30 June 1523. The clergy were asked to lend a quarter of their annual income and of the value of their goods. The bishops and prelates produced £38,000, the general clergy £18,000, or a total of £56,000, close to Wolsey's estimate of £60,000. In total the loan amounted to the quite fantastic sum of £260,000.[60]

In order to place this in perspective, it is necessary to compare it with the proceeds of taxation in the 1510s. The four fifteenths and tenths paid in 1512, 1513, 1514 and 1517 each yielded about £29,500. The subsidies paid in the mid-1510s produced £32,500 in 1513, £49,500 in 1514, £44,900 in 1515 and £44,000 in 1516. Total lay taxation in the mid-1510s was therefore some £287,000 spread over five years.[61] The sum of £204,000 raised from the laity by the loan of 1522–3 in a single year reflects a far greater annual rate. The clergy had paid a tenth in 1513, 1514, 1515 and 1516, and half a tenth in 1517, 1518, 1519 and 1520. A tenth usually yielded between £11,000 and £12,000, except for the final two half-tenths which together produced just £9,620. The clergy, then, paid some £66,000 in taxation in the years 1515 to 1520. The sum of £57,000 raised by the loan of 1522 in a single year was again at a vastly greater rate.[62]

The loan of 1522–3 was a remarkable fiscal and political achievement by Henry VIII and Wolsey. There was some disquiet expressed in Kent. Archbishop Warham had not only promised that it would be repaid but (according to a later petition addressed to him) had agreed that if it were not he would repay it himself.[63] There was some opposition in London, where before the great loan the city had been asked to lend £30,000 (it agreed to £20,000 under Wolsey's threats and the imprisonment of certain refusers) in the spring and a further 4,000 marks in September.[64] These earlier demands must have reinforced the impact of the great loan in London, producing an atmosphere of complaints against financial exactions and consequent impoverishment, and against wasteful government spending, that permeates John Skelton's *Why Come Ye Not to Court*, written after 28 October 1522 by a poet in search of metropolitan mercantile patronage.[65] In August the Venetian ambassador reported that the whole population of England was dissatisfied with the war because they were made to pay.[66] But it is vital to note that the loan was paid. It is misleading to claim that the country 'exhibited signs of acute disorder over a loan for the wars' or that the political costs of the loan were considerable.[67] It was paid with resignation as much as with grudging.[68] Of course it was a loan, not a tax, and it was due for repayment from the proceeds of the next parliamentary grant: during the parliament of 1523 Wolsey promised 'on his feithe that the ij^s of the li of lone money shalbe payed with a good will and with thanke', though without appointing a date.[69] But it was impossible for taxation at the levels of the 1510s to produce anything like enough to repay the loan speedily. In the event the loan was not repaid: it was cancelled by an act of parliament in 1529. Its vast size and the fact that it had not been repaid must, however, be borne in mind in assessing reactions to the Amicable Grant.

In 1523 parliament was summoned and asked to grant taxation for the crown. Wolsey initially asked for a rate of 4s. in the £ (20%) on goods and lands which he (extravagantly) claimed would raise £800,000.[70] This was an obvious bargaining position. In 1512 Warham, Wolsey's predecessor as Lord Chancellor, had shown the commons that the king wanted to invade France: 'he askyth of the commnys vi^c thosonde pownde for to meynteyne the warys one yere', before settling for rates which produced £126,745.[71] Wolsey's request provoked much argument. A correspondent of the earl of Surrey noted on 14 May

the grettiste and soreste hold in the Lower Hous for paymente . . . that ever was sene I think in any parliamente. This matier hathe been debated and beaten xv or xvi dayes to gidder. . . . There hathe bene suche hold that the Hous was like to have bene dissevered.[72]

There was some popular opposition too: at Whitsuntide 'the common people saied to the burgesses, sirs, we heare saie that you will graunt iiii^s of the pound, we aduise you to do so that ye maie go home, with many euill woordes and threatenynges'.[73] After discussion the commons granted a subsidy at rates lower than those which Wolsey had first sought. It would be wrong, however, to criticise Wolsey for mismanagement, or to describe the behaviour of the commons as 'widespread, determined and in the end successful' opposition. Here it is crucial to note the conventions of bargaining over the rates at which taxation was voted. There is no evidence to support the argument that before Whitsun the commons offered the reduced rates described by Edward Hall only to lower their offer still further after the Whitsun recess to the rates listed in the statute. There is no evidence that Wolsey turned down an offer higher than that which he ultimately accepted; no evidence that the rates offered were reduced after Whitsun.[74]

According to the statute, the subsidy was to be levied at the rate of 2s. in the £ (10%) spread over two years, thus making 1s. in the £ (5%) in each year, from those with lands, or goods worth over £20; at the rate of 1s. in the £ (5%) over two years, or 6d. in the £ ($2^1/_2$%) in each year, from those with goods worth between £2 and £20; with a flat charge of 4d. in each year for those worth £2 in goods or £1 in wages. In addition, those with lands worth more than £50 would pay a further 1s. in the £ (5%) in the third year, those with goods worth more than £50 would pay a further 1s. in the £ (5%) in the fourth year.[75]

Surrey's correspondent claimed that 'I have herd no man yn my lif that can remembre that ever ther was geven to any oon of the Kings auncestours half so moche at oon graunte; nor I thinke ther was never suche a president sene before this tyme'.[76] Cromwell wrote that 'we haue in our parlyament grauntyd unto the Kinges highnes a right large subsydye, the lyke wherof was neuer grauntyd in this realme'.[77] These opinions were not quite correct. The combined subsidy and fifteenths and tenths of the mid-1510s had produced slightly larger sums than the subsidy of 1523 would. The lay loan of 1522–3 had, moreover, been vastly greater. But the perception of contemporaries is perhaps more significant than the precise figures calculated by the modern historian in explaining why in 1525 there was such reluctance to make a further grant. It is interesting that these comments stressed the size of the subsidy granted by the commons rather than the way in which any supposed opposition had forced Wolsey to reduce his demands. And the sums raised by the 1523 subsidy — £72,000 in the first instalment in 1524, £64,000 in the second instalment in 1525 — were certainly large amounts.[78] Of that first instalment, between £15,500 and £20,000 — estimates vary — was asked for and paid in 'anticipation' in autumn 1523, during the military campaigns of that year.[79] Increasing delays in payment point to the growing weariness of taxpayers. 74% of the anticipation was paid within one month of the date fixed, 47% of the first instalment of the subsidy, but only 19% of the second instalment.[80] Some discontent was expressed. Surrey's correspondent in May besought God that the subsidy might be 'well and peasibly levied', thinking that the gentlemen whose task it would be to levy it 'shal have no litle besynes aboute the same'.[81] In 1523 one Peter Wilkinson of Norfolk thought it would be better to take against King Henry than that they should pay taxes.[82] There was a mysterious plot later that year in which Francis Philip, schoolmaster to the king's 'Henxmen', Christopher Pickering, clerk of the larder, and one Anthony Manyvile, gentleman, 'entended to haue taken the kynges treasure of his subsidie, as the collectours of the same came towarde London, and then to haue raised men and taken the castle of Kylingworth, and then to haue made battaile against the kyng'. These three were hanged, drawn and quartered at

Tyburn in February 1524: 'the residue that were taken were sent to the citie of Coventry, and ther wer executed'.[83] De Praet, the imperial ambassador, alluded to this in January as a 'kind of mutiny' when writing about the parliamentary subsidy. He somewhat inaccurately said that the subsidy had not yet been raised and that many thought that it would provoke considerable disorder.[84] This was not the only occasion in 1524 that he noted disquiet over taxation. In March he thought that unless the king would either win a victory or make peace, that is unless he followed a definite policy, he would fail to get the money that had been voted or face a rebellion from some part of his people.[85] In May he thought that the counsellors would find the people disinclined to continue the war and to pay the sums granted to the king the previous year. All the people of all estates were weary of the cost of the war, that is wearied by royal financial demands.[86] In August he wrote in similar vein: all classes were wearied of the war on account of the heavy taxes.[87] It is not surprising that the Amicable Grant, against such a background, was to meet with resistance.

The church had also been persuaded to grant heavy taxation in 1523. This was to be paid at the rate of 10s. in the £ (50%), spread over five years, thus making 2s. in the £ (10%) a year, on revenues from £8 upwards; at the rate of 6s. 8d. in the £ (33⅓%), or 1s. 4d. in the £ (6⅔%) a year, on revenues of £8 downwards; with a special rate of 5s. in the £ (25%), or 1s. in the £ (5%) a year, on those specially exempted from higher rates on grounds of extreme poverty.[88] No details of the receipts survive,[89] but Wolsey calculated that the grant would produce £120,000, or £24,000 p.a. This compares with £11,000–£12,000 p.a. in the mid-1510s, and with the £56,000 raised in the single year of the 1522 loan.[90] The clergy were making the second instalment of this subsidy when they were faced by the new demand of the Amicable Grant. It is not surprising that they were prominent in refusing, complaining, in Kent, that the king had had an annual tenth for sixteen years and that the church had never been so continually charged.[91]

Men's sense of being poor is, of course, relative. It is difficult to assess the precise impact of taxation, especially on the poor. Writing of the 1523 subsidy, the editors of the roll for Buckinghamshire could opine that 'it is to be doubted if the levying of it caused any real hardship'.[92] A student of an earlier period could suggest that taxation in the late 1410s 'at its worst' threw on the country 'an average burden per head equivalent to three and one half days' wages for a carpenter at the maximum wage'.[93] By modern standards the rates at which taxes were raised are puny. But such assessments may be too sanguine. Poorer men did not hold reserves from which to pay royal demands. Taxation followed on demands from landlords and the church. Above all the impact of taxation could be cumulative. It may well be that the demand of an Amicable Grant was resented not so much because of absolute, desperate, poverty but because it came hard on years of financial levies which were themselves at an unprecedented scale. By past standards the demands on the laity and clergy in 1522–5 had been remarkably high. Many may by 1525 have sincerely felt impoverished and it is reasonable to suppose that repeated payments made from fluctuating annual income may have caused real difficulties. A frequent claim in 1525 was that men were not now as well off as the valuations of 1522 (which were to be used for the Amicable Grant) suggested. Many in Kent offered less than what was demanded, explaining that this more exactly corresponded to their current worth, alleging great poverty and decay in their goods.[94] Many in Cambridgeshire and the Isle of Ely said that they had suffered losses by fire and murrain. Those before valued at £100 or £200 could not now make 20 nobles in cash, scarcely 40s. Some who were well off at the time of the loan in 1522 were not now worth a groat once what they owed was reckoned up.[95] In London one alderman protested to Wolsey that 'sithe the last valuation [of 1522] diuerse merchantes be decaied by the seas, and suretiship, and other waies, so that valuacion cannot bee had', a protest Wolsey tacitly accepted.[96] Others said they had deliberately overstated their wealth in 1522 in order to advance or to maintain their credit: presumably these must have been specially hard hit by the loan and subsidy.[97]

And if the loans of 1522–3 had raised unprecedented sums, and if the subsidy granted in 1523 and payable in 1524 and 1525 was also yielding record sums, it is worth noting that the Amicable Grant, had it been successful, would have produced still more. That it could have succeeded seems inconceivable in the light of the pattern, or of what might be proposed as the law, of diminishing returns of medieval taxation. A government could demand vast sums, and secure them, in one year; but if it persisted, the yields fell and took longer to secure, and resistance, in parliament, in passive refusals, in outright rebellion grew, forcing the reduction, abandonment and (for a period) the cessation of demands. Such a pattern can be found not only in the early 1520s and mid-1510s but also in all the periods of substantial royal financial demands in late medieval England: between 1290 and 1297, 1336 and 1341, 1371 and 1381, 1417 and 1422.[98]

In 1290 Edward I's government was able to raise the astonishing sum of £116,000 (possibly unmatched since the pre-Conquest danegeld) by a fifteenth sanctioned in parliament and paid by the laity.[99] The tenth and sixth agreed in 1294 produced some £82,000, a sharp reduction, although still a remarkable yield.[100] But each successive lay subsidy thereafter, in 1295, 1296 and 1297, produced less than its predecessor: £53,000 in 1295, £38,000 in 1296, while the last in this annual series, the ninth of 1297, produced least of all (just £34,000), though imposed at the highest rate. As the methods of the government became increasingly arbitrary, resistance grew into constitutional crisis and the remonstrances of 1297.[101] The consequence was a notable reduction in the size and the frequency of royal fiscal demands for many years: the yield of parliamentary taxes remained well below even that of 1295, let alone those of 1290 and 1294.[102]

Not until the late 1330s did a government again attempt to raise very large sums of money. At first Edward III succeeded: in 1337 parliament granted a fifteenth and tenth not just for one but for three successive years, yielding £114,000 in total.[103] One historian has seen the combined burdens of heavy taxation, extensive purveyance and experiments to increase customs dues paid on wool as producing a period of greater royal demands on the peasantry in the late 1330s than the 1290s or the years before 1381.[104] However that may be, the weight of the fiscal demands can be gauged from the delayed parliamentary offer in 1339 not of a further fifteenth and tenth but of a tax in kind, the ninth sheaf, lamb and fleece, and from the failure of this tax to produce more than £15,000 in a year (less than half the yield of a fifteenth and tenth), largely as a result of passive resistance, a striking reversal for the government.[105] In a climate marked by popular verses against taxation, there were some signs both of fears of rebellion and of risks of a political and constitutional crisis. However slight the likelihood of serious disturbance may have been, political discontent was increasing, and it is significant that the government made various concessions, over purveyance and the misdeeds of royal ministers, and showed considerable restraint in its fiscal demands in the 1340s.[106]

The English rising of 1381 followed a decade of heavy financial demands. Sizeable parliamentary subsidies had been granted in 1372 and 1373 (a single followed by a double fifteenth and tenth yielding £113,000 over three years) and again (after resistance in 1376) in 1377 and 1380 (a double fifteenth and tenth followed by a fifteenth and tenth and a half, yielding £133,000).[107] Moreover governments were experimenting with various schemes of taxing people rather than property, perhaps in itself a reflection of growing resistance to traditional forms of taxation. The poll tax of 1377 was disappointing in producing just £23,000, yet sufficiently effective for the government to think it worth further attempts.[108] The second poll tax produced somewhat less, £19,000.[109] Unwisely the government tried again in late 1380, trebling the basic rate per head from 4d. to a shilling.[110] This demand, which would have produced £66,000 in a single year,[111] met with evasion (though some £44,000 was collected):[112] a third of those who had paid in 1377 did not pay in 1381.[113] Moreover the government's methods in trying to ensure payment triggered off a large-scale rebellion in June 1381.[114] Its primarily fiscal causes appear sufficiently clearly in the Commons' reluctance to grant further taxation in the parliaments after the rising.[115] Once again there had proved to be a limit to the taxation that a government could secure.

This pattern of initial success followed by increasing resistance may also be seen in the reign of Henry V. Henry V was able to raise huge sums from 1414, especially between 1415 and early 1417, including two subsidies in a single year (bringing some £75,000 in to the exchequer in 1415 and £50,000 in 1416),[116] but soon difficulties appeared. A general loan authorised by parliament in 1419 yielded practically nothing.[117] In November 1419 the Commons granted just one fifteenth and tenth and a further third of a fifteenth and tenth. 'They had reached their limit'. Nothing was asked for in December 1420 and nothing obtained in 1421 until December (despite a meeting of parliament in May which may have been stormy).[118] Growing war-weariness was evident by 1420 in Yorkshire where very few gentlemen were willing to provide further military service.[119] Significantly the government had recourse to widespread borrowing in 1421, securing some £36,000, though even so the city of London was willing to lend far less than earlier, and much of the total came from a few individuals; significantly too parliament refused to grant money to repay these loans.[120] Adam of Usk wrote how 'in truth the grievous taxation of the people' was 'unbearable, accompanied with murmurs and with smothered curses among them from hatred of the burden'.[121] Most pointedly of all, after December 1421 no new direct taxation was granted until 1429.

The pattern of initial generosity followed by increasing resistance and dwindling yields may also be observed in the reign of Henry VI, although it is complicated by the repeated and urgent demands of a defensive war and, in the late 1440s, by political strife, and by doubts about the competence and commitment of the government. In 1429 the commons granted, generously, a double fifteenth and tenth,[122] in 1431 they were willing to experiment with a tax on income from land;[123] but by 1432 they were willing to offer just half a fifteenth and tenth,[124] from 1433 they began to reduce the yield of fifteenths and tenths by making allowances for poverty (increased in the 1440s).[125] Between 1428 and 1436 £207,821 was raised in lay taxation; between 1436 and 1453, a longer period, and one of greater military need, only £239,500 was secured.[126] The income tax of 1436 produced just £9,000.[127] From the mid-1440s the commons granted little: only one-half of a fifteenth and tenth in 1445,[128] nothing in 1447,[129] a half in the first session of 1449, nothing in the second, another half in the third,[130] and then in 1450 another tax on income from land that failed.[131] One of the complaints in Cade's rebellion was heavy taxation, reflecting the cumulative burdens of the previous decades.[132] Not surprisingly, there was little taxation on a sustained scale under the Yorkists and consequently no fiscal difficulties, although Edward's demands in the early 1470s might, if they had continued, have provoked discontent.

Further signs of a pattern of diminishing fiscal returns may be seen in the 1510s. At first Henry VIII did secure very large sums. There was no doubt some bargaining in parliament in 1512 over the rates,[133] but heavy taxes were paid. Moreover the form of these taxes was significant: a poll tax was offered in 1513, the first since 1381, and the subsidy of 1513, based on an assessment of personal wealth, was successfully carried through. To begin with, a government could secure large sums by reformed means. But soon problems mounted. In early 1514 the Commons granted £160,000 to be paid on 24 June 1514 but only some £51,000 was raised; a further £110,000 was granted in February 1515 but by November 1515 only £46,000 had been paid; a new subsidy for 1516 and a fifteenth and tenth for 1517 were voted then.[134] Lay taxation thus yielded £51,000 in 1514, £46,000 in 1515 and £45,000 in 1516. 'The reduction in yield may well reflect a certain resistance to the continued demands of the crown'.[135] By 1516 arrears had mounted in assessments of the city of London. Wolsey believed that assessments were fraudulent; aldermen were not prepared to swear to them.[136] By 1519–20 the yield of a clerical tenth had fallen from £11,000–£12,000 to just £9,620.[137] Hall writes a great deal about the exactions of the early 1520s, for which he is a principal source, but much less about those of the 1510s, creating a misleading impression that there were no tensions in the 1510s. He makes no comment at all about the taxes granted in January 1512, and November–December 1512, is bland about the taxes of late 1514–15 — 'dyuerse subsidies were graunted to the kynge towarde hys greate costes and charges, that he had bene at in his vyage royall in Fraunce' — and does not mention the taxation granted in November 1515 at all.[138] But careful reading of the evidence points to increasing problems and diminishing returns in the mid-to-late 1510s. The early 1520s were no exception to the rule. The striking success of the loan of 1522–3 and of the large subsidy granted in 1523 could not be sustained: it is not surprising that the remarkable achievements of 1522–23 resulted in the remarkable failure of 1525. In the early 1520s, as in 1336–41, and the other periods reviewed above, 'taxation was cumulative in its oppressive effects'.[139]

What broader economic evidence is there to suggest that royal demands were likely to impose heavy burdens in 1525? Was fiscal oppression superimposed on increasing economic hardship? Were there any economic circumstances in that year, or in immediately preceding years, or any special regional difficulties, that justified cries of poverty? There is nothing in national grain price series to show that bad harvests, or high grain prices, were responsible for the difficulties of 1525. The average for all grains which had been as high as 193 in 1520 and 183 in 1521 was just 116 in 1522, 110 in 1523, 116 in 1524 and 110 in 1525.[140] Even allowing for the possibility that coin shortage depressed prices,[141] it would be difficult to argue from these figures that there was any impoverishment arising from bad harvests. If population trends in the early sixteenth century are not agreed, it does nonetheless seem safe to say that agricultural evidence does not point to any significant pressure on land at this time.[142] There were certainly significant outbreaks of plague between 1518–23.[143] But mortality rates were not as high in the early and mid-1520s as they were to be in the late 1550s or the mid-1590s. This was not a period of desperate hardship caused by disease and bad weather.

Customs records of the exports of wool show a quite marked reduction in the early 1520s in exports from London and particularly from Boston but it is difficult to connect this decline with the refusals of 1525.[144] Exports of cloth from London and Ipswich dipped in 1520–21 but soon recovered; exports from Yarmouth fell away quite sharply in 1522–25. This is inconclusive.[145] Wool prices, however, do suggest the possibility of a slump. The price series stood above 100 in every year between 1508 and 1522 — 117 in 1520, 103 in 1521, 122 in 1522 — but then fell to 94 in 1523 and 96 in 1524 before recovering to 119 in 1525.[146] Could some of the difficulties in the Suffolk clothing towns, where insurrection took place in 1525, be at least in part the consequence of a temporary fall in wool prices, itself brought about by a reduced demand for clothing as men paid the loan of 1522–3 and the instalments of the subsidy voted in 1523 and due in 1524 and 1525? This can only be speculative. But it indicates that a closer investigation of the troubles in Suffolk, and of the clothiers and textile industry there, may shed further light on the question of poverty and the Amicable Grant.

Notes

1 B.L. Cotton MS, Cleopatra F vi fo. 339 (Ellis, *Original Letters,* 3rd series, i. 369; *LP,* IV, i 1243).

2 Hall, *Chronicle,* p. 696.

3 B.L. Cotton MS, Titus B i fos. 273–273ᵛ (*LP,* IV, i 1267).

4 PRO SP1/34/fo. 198 (*LP,* IV, i 1330). Quotation is not in *LP.*

5 B.L. Cotton MS, Cleopatra F vi fo. 348 (Ellis, *Original Letters,* 3rd series, i. 362–3, 365; *LP,* IV, i 1266).

6 B.L. Cotton MS, Cleopatra F vi fo. 339 (Ellis, *Original Letters,* 3rd series, i. 371; *LP,* IV, i 1243).

7 B.L. Cotton MS, Titus B i fo. 271 (*LP,* IV, i 1272).

8 Hall, *Chronicle,* p. 700, Cf. 'The weaver declared that they knew no captain other than Poverty' (*HMC, Wales,* i. p. iv); cf. A.G. Dickens, ed., *The Register or Chronicle of Butley Priory, Suffolk 1510–35* (Winchester, 1951), p. 48.

9 G.L. Harriss, 'Aids, loans and benevolences', *Historical Journal,* vi (1963), pp. 16–17; 'Thomas Cromwell's "new principle" of taxation', *English Historical Review,* xciii (1978), pp. 721–38 esp. 721–4; 'Theory and practice in royal taxation: some observations', *English Historical Review,* xcvii (1982), pp. 811–19 esp. pp. 811–12; 'Medieval doctrines in the debates on supply', in K.M. Sharpe, ed., *Faction and Parliament: essays on early Stuart history* (1978), pp. 73–103; *King, Parliament and Public Finance in Medieval England to 1369* (Oxford, 1975).

10 B.L. Cotton MS, Cleopatra F vi fo. 339ᵛ (Ellis, *Original Letters,* 3rd series, i 371–2; *LP,* IV, i 1243).

11 B.L. Cotton MS, Cleopatra F vi fo. 347ᵛ (Ellis, *Original Letters,* 3rd series, i. 361; *LP,* IV, i 1266).

12 B.L. Cotton MS, Titus B i fo. 273 (*LP,* IV, i 1267).

13 PRO SP1/34/fo. 185 (*LP,* IV, i 1311).

14 B.L. Cotton MS, Cleopatra F vi fo. 337 (Ellis, *Original Letters,* 3rd series, i. 378–9; *LP,* IV, i 1235).

15 B.L. Cotton MS, Cleopatra F vi fos. 348–348ᵛ (Ellis, *Original Letters,* 3rd series, i. 363, 365; *LP,* IV, i 1266).

16 B.L. Cotton MS, Vespasian F xvii fo. 133b (*LP,* IV, i 1305).

17 PRO SP1/234/fo. 240 (*LP,* appendix 457).

18 PRO SP1/34/fo. 173 (*LP,* IV, i 1306).

19 B.L. Cotton MS, Titus B i fo. 271ᵛ (*LP,* IV, i 1272).

20 Hall, *Chronicle,* p. 696, cf. p. 698.

21 *Ibid.,* p. 700.

22 B.L. Cotton MS, Cleopatra F vi fos. 337ᵛ (Ellis, *Original Letters,* 3rd series, i. 380; *LP,* IV, i 1235).

23 *HMC, Wales*, i. p. v.
24 Corporation of London Records Office, Letter Book N fos. 278–278ᵛ. Cf. Coventry Record Office, A 79 i 55.
25 Hall, *Chronicle*, p. 698.
26 *Ibid.*, pp. 700–1.
27 *State Papers*, iii no. xviii p. 67 (I owe this reference to Mr P.J. Gwyn).
28 Hall, *Chronicle*, p. 698.
29 *Ibid.*, p. 697.
30 *Ibid.*, p. 699.
31 B.L. Cotton MS, Cleopatra F vi fo. 341ᵛ (Ellis, *Original Letters*, 3rd series, ii. 10; *LP*, IV, i 1332).
32 B.L. Cotton MS, Cleopatra F vi fos. 337–8 (Ellis, *Original Letters*, 3rd series, i. 379–81; *LP*, IV, i 1235); C.E. Challis, *The Tudor Coinage* (Manchester, 1978), pp. 66–8.
33 B.L. Cotton MS, Titus B i fo. 271ᵛ (*LP*, IV, 1272).
34 B.L. Cotton MS, Vespasian F xiii fo. 133b (*LP*, IV, i 1305).
35 PRO SP1/234/fo. 240 (*LP*, appendix 457).
36 B.L. Cotton MS, Cleopatra F vi fos. 339ᵛ–340 (Ellis, *Original Letters*, 3rd series, i. 373–4; *LP*, IV, i 1243).
37 *LP*, IV, i 1567.
38 B.L. Cotton MS, Titus B i fo. 272 (*LP*, IV, i 1272).
39 Hall, *Chronicle*, p. 693.
40 *LP*, IV, 951; *Cal. S.P., Spanish, F.S.*, pp. 418, 433; *Cal. S.P., Spanish*, iii (i) no. 46 pp. 94–5.
41 Ellis, *Original Letters*, 3rd series, i. 373 (*LP*, IV i 1243).
42 Challis, *Tudor Coinage*, pp. 67–71, 166, 169, 221–2, and cf. pp. 157, 202; J.F. Larkin and P.L. Hughes, *Tudor Royal Proclamations* (3 vols., 1964–9), i. 136, 141.
43 Schofield, thesis cit., p. 289.
44 Hall, *Chronicle*, p. 656; Challis, *Tudor Coinage*, p. 236.
45 B.L. Cotton MS, Cleopatra F vi fo. 339 (Ellis, *Original Letters*, 3rd series, i. 371; *LP*, IV, i 1243).
46 *HMC, Wales*, i. p. iv.
47 Hall, *Chronicle*, p. 699.
48 *Ibid.*, p. 698.
49 *HMC, Wales*, i. p. iii.
50 Schofield, thesis cit., table 41, pp. 431–2.
51 PRO SP1/34/fo. 192 (*LP*, IV, i 1321).
52 B.L. Cotton MS, Cleopatra F vi fo. 339 (Ellis, *Original Letters*, 3rd series, i. 370; *LP*, IV, i 1243).
53 *Statutes of the Realm*, iii. 44, 74–5, 105–6, 163–4, 195–7.
54 Hall, *Chronicle*, p. 697.
55 B.L. Cotton MS, Cleopatra F vi fo. 339ᵛ (Ellis, *Original Letters*, 3rd series, i. 372; *LP*, IV, i 1243).
56 B.L. Cotton MS, Cleopatra F vi fo. 348 (Ellis, *Original Letters*, 1st series, i. 364; *LP*, IV i 1266).
57 J.J. Goring, 'The general proscription of 1522', *English Historical Review*, lxxxvi (1971), pp. 681–705.

58 Hall, *Chronicle*, p. 645; *LP*, III, ii 2484.

59 *LP*, III, ii 2895.

60 PRO SP1/25/fo. 190 (*LP*, III, ii 2483 (3)); PRO E36/221/fos. 6, 7^v, 9, 14, 17^v (IV, i 214); B.L. Cotton MS, Cleopatra F vi fo. 340^v (*LP*, IV, iii appendix 37).

61 Schofield, table 40, pp. 415–16.

62 Kelly, thesis cit., p. 301.

63 PRO SP1/47/fo. 191 (not in *LP*, IV ii 4173).

64 Hall, *Chronicle*, pp. 642, 650; J. Kennedy, 'The city of London and the crown c.1509–c.1529', University of Manchester M.A. thesis, 1978, pp. 148–50.

65 G. Walker, ' "Baytyngg the Bochers dogg": the satires of John Skelton against Cardinal Wolsey as a source for the politics of the 1520s', University of Southampton Ph.D. thesis, 1985, ch. iii part iii.

66 *Cal. S.P., Venetian*, no. 537 p. 270.

67 R.L. Woods, 'Politics and precedent: Wolsey's parliament of 1523', *Huntington Library Quarterly*, xl (1976–7), p. 301; Goring, *loc. cit.*, p. 702.

68 Cf. tone of Hall, *Chronicle*, p. 650.

69 Ellis, *Original Letters*, 1st series, i. 221 (*LP*, III ii 3024).

70 Hall, *Chronicle*, pp. 655–6.

71 W.C. and C.E. Trevelyan, eds., *Trevelyan Papers, iii., Camden Society*, cv (1872), p. 8.

72 B.L. Cotton MS, Titus B i fo. 112 (Ellis, *Original Letters*, 1st series, i. 220; *LP*, III ii 3024). Cf. M.M. Rowe, ed., 'Tudor Exeter: tax assessments 1489–1595 including the military survey 1522', *Devonshire and Cornwall Record Society*, new series, xxii (1977), p. xiii ('The moste part of the lower or common house grudged and murmured').

73 Hall, *Chronicle*, p., 657.

74 Schofield, thesis cit., pp. 33–6, 39; cf. Kennedy, thesis cit., p. 149.

75 *Statutes of the Realm*, iii. 231.

76 B.L. Cotton MS, Titus B i fo. 112 (Ellis, *Original Letters*, 1st series, i. 221; *LP*, III ii 3024).

77 Merriman, *Life and Letters of Thomas Cromwell*, i. 313; *LP*, III, ii 3249.

78 Schofield, table 40, pp. 415–16. Wolsey expected the first payment of the subsidy to be £68,000 (PRO SP1/25/fo. 190 (*LP*, III, ii 2483)).

79 Hall, *Chronicle*, p. 672; PRO SP1/25/fo. 190 (*LP*, III, ii 2483); *LP*, III ii 3504.

80 Schofield, table 41, pp. 431–2. Schofield (p. 435) says that the fact that only 5% of the anticipation was paid by the date set shows that it was ineffective — but 74% was paid within a further month.

81 Ellis, *Original Letters*, 1st series, i. 221 (*LP*, III, ii 3024).

82 *LP*, III, ii 3802.

83 Hall, *Chronicle*, p. 673; LP, IV, ii 2751.

84 *Cal. S.P., Spanish, F.S.*, pp. 301–2.

85 *Ibid.*, p. 319.

86 *Ibid.*, p. 354.

87 *Ibid.*, pp. 369–70.

88 Kelly, thesis cit., p. 308; Polydore Vergil, pp. 306–7.

89 Kelly, thesis cit., pp. 311–12.

90 PRO SP1/25/fo. 190 (*LP*, III, ii 2483 (3)). Was there opposition in convocation as (only) Vergil suggests: Polydore Vergil, pp. 306–7; cf. Kelly, thesis cit., pp. 174–5; Heath, *loc. cit.*, pp. 101–9.

91 B.L. Cotton MS, Titus B i fos. 273–4 (*LP*, IV i 1267).

92 A.C. Chibnall and A. Vere Woodman, 'Subsidy roll for the county of Buckingham anno 1524', *Buckinghamshire Record Society*, viii (1950), p. xv.

93 R.A. Newhall, 'The war finances of Henry V and the duke of Bedford', *English Historical Review*, xxxvi (1921), p. 197.

94 B.L. Cotton MS, Cleopatra F vi fo. 348 (Ellis, *Original Letters*, 3rd series, i. 359–67; *LP*, IV, i 1266).

95 B.L. Cotton MS, Titus B i fos. 271–72ᵛ (*LP*, IV, i 1272).

96 Hall, *Chronicle*, p. 696.

97 *Ibid.*, p. 697; cf. National Library of Wales, Aberystwyth, NLW MS 3054 D (Mostyn 158), pp. 476b–77b (I am most grateful to Mr Huw Roberts of the NLW for translating these pages for me).

98 I should specially wish to acknowledge the generous guidance of my colleague Mr T.B. Pugh on the problems discussed in the following pages. I am also grateful to Dr M.C. Carpenter and Dr G.L. Harriss for scrutinising a late draft. In stressing the theme of diminishing returns I am of course aware of the need to consider other factors such as constitutional concerns, political circumstances, the competence of particular governments, attitudes to the aims and methods of foreign policy, but I should claim that only a pattern of diminishing returns can explain both why governments did initially manage to raise vast sums and why they had increasing difficulties if they continued to try to do so.

99 J.F. Willard, *Parliamentary taxes on personal property 1290 to 1334: a study in mediaeval English financial administration* (Cambridge, Mass., 1934), pp. 343–4; G.L. Harriss, *King, Parliament and Public Finance in medieval England to 1369* (Oxford, 1975), p. 41. (I have not attempted to convert sums of money raised by late medieval taxation into constant £s.)

100 Willard, *Parliamentary taxes*, pp. 343–4; E.B. Fryde, 'Financial resources of Edward I in the Netherlands, 1294–98: main problems and some comparisons with Edward III in 1337–40', *Revue belge de philologie et d'histoire*, xl (1962), p. 1173.

101 Willard, *Parliamentary taxes*, pp. 343–5; Fryde, 'Financial resources', pp. 1173–4; E.B. Fryde, 'The financial policies of the royal governments and popular resistance to them in France and England c.1270–c.1420', *Revue Belge de philologie et d'histoire*, lvii (1979), p. 832 (reprinted in *Studies in Medieval Trade and Finance* (1983), ch. I); E. Miller, 'War, taxation and the English economy in the late thirteenth and early fourteenth centuries', in J.M. Winter, ed., *War and economic development: essays in memory of David Joslin* (Cambridge, 1975), pp. 11–12, 15, 21.

102 Willard, *Parliamentary taxes*, pp. 343–5.

103 J.R. Maddicott, *The English peasantry and the demands of the crown, Past and Present, supplement*, i (1975), p. 46; M. Prestwich, *The three Edwards: war and state in England 1277–1377* (1980), p. 216.

104 Maddicott, *English peasantry*, pp. 45, 64–67.

105 N.M. Fryde, 'Edward III's removal of his ministers and judges, 1340–1', *Bulletin of the Institute of Historical Research*, xlviii (1975), p. 152; Prestwich, *Three Edwards*, 217–18.

106 Maddicott, *English peasantry*, pp. 64–67; Fryde, 'Financial policies', pp. 839–40; Harriss, *King, Parliament and Public Finance*, p. 234.

107 J.W. Sherborne, 'The cost of English warfare with France in the later fourteenth century', *Bulletin of the Institute of Historical Research*, l (1977), pp. 141, 149; Fryde, 'Financial policies', p. 852; *ex inf.* Dr G.L. Harriss and Mr T.B. Pugh.

108 E.B. Fryde, 'Parliament and the peasants' revolt of 1381', in *Liber Memorialis George de Lagarde* (Louvain), (reprinted in *Studies in Medieval Trade and Finance*, ch. XIII) p. 78; *The Great Revolt of 1381* (Historical Association pamphlet, c, 1981), p. 11.

109 Fryde, 'Parliament', p. 77; *Great Revolt*, p. 11

110 Fryde, 'Parliament', pp. 78–9.

111 *Ibid.*, pp. 77–78; *Great Revolt*, p. 11.

112 Fryde, *Great Revolt*, p. 15

113 *Ibid.*, p. 11.

114 Maddicott, *English peasantry*, p. 66; Fryde, *Great Revolt*, p. 7.

115 J.A. Tuck, 'Nobles, commons and the great revolt of 1381', in R.H. Hilton and T.H. Aston, eds., *The English Rising of 1381* (Cambridge, 1984), pp. 204, 208; N. Brooks, 'The organisation and achievements of the peasants of Kent and Essex in 1381', in H. Mayr-Harting and R.I. Moore, eds., *Studies in Medieval History presented to R.H.C. Davis*, (1985), pp. 262–5, 270; R.B. Dobson, 'Remembering the peasants' revolt 1381–1981', in W.H. Liddell and R.G.E. Wood, eds., *Essex and the Great Revolt of 1381* (Essex, 1982), pp. 7, 18; J.R. Maddicott, *Law and Lordship: royal justices as retainers in thirteenth and fourteenth century England, Past and Present, supplement*, iv (1978), pp. 70–1; Fryde, *Great Revolt*, p. 34; G.L. Harriss, 'The management of parliament', in G.L. Harriss, ed., *Henry V: the practice of kingship* (Oxford, 1985), p. 146.

116 Newhall, 'War finances of Henry V', pp. 173, 175; Harriss, 'Parliament', p. 145.

117 G.L. Harriss, 'Financial policy', in Harriss, ed., *Henry V*, p. 166.

118 Harriss, 'Parliament', pp. 149–50; 'Financial policy', p. 167.

119 A.E. Goodman, 'Responses to requests in Yorkshire for military service under Henry V', *Northern History*, xvii (1981), pp. 243–7, 250.

120 Harriss, 'Financial policy', pp. 165–6; Newhall, 'War finances of Henry V', p. 175.

121 E.M. Thompson, ed., *Chronicon Adae de Usk* (2nd edn., 1904), p. 320; cf. D. McCulloch and E.D. Jones, 'Lancastrian politics, the French war and the rise of the popular element', *Speculum*, lviii (i) (1983), p. 100.

122 R.A. Griffiths, *The reign of Henry VI: the exercise of royal authority 1422–1461* (1981), p. 116.

123 Griffiths, *Henry VI*, p. 117; R. Virgoe, 'The parliamentary subsidy of 1450', *Bulletin of the Institute of Historical Research*, lv (1982), p. 127.

124 Griffiths, *Henry VI*, p. 117.

125 *Ibid.;* Virgoe, 'Parliamentary subsidy of 1450', pp. 127–8.

126 Griffiths, *Henry VI*, pp. 110, 384.

127 *Ibid.*, p. 118.

128 *Ibid.*, p. 380.

129 *Ibid.*

130 *Ibid.*; Virgoe, 'Parliamentary subsidy of 1450', p. 128.

131 Griffiths, *Henry VI*, p. 381; Virgoe, 'Parliamentary subsidy of 1450', pp. 125–38.

132 Griffiths, *Henry VI*, pp. 635–6.

133 The poll tax of 1512 may initially have been sought at the rate of 1s. not the actual 4d: C.M. Woolgar, *A Catalogue of the estate archives of St Mary Magdalen College, Oxford*, n.d., p. 80 (I owe this reference to Mr R.W. Hoyle).

134 *Statutes of the Realm*, iii, 105–6, 163–4, 195–7.

135 Schofield, thesis cit., pp. 426, 439.

136 Hall, *Chronicle*, p. 585; Kennedy, thesis cit., pp. 138–41.

137 Kelly, thesis cit., p. 301.

138 Hall, *Chronicle*, pp. 526, 535, 581.

139 Maddicott, *English peasantry*, p. 53.

140 P. Bowden, 'Statistical appendix', in J. Thirsk, ed., *The Agrarian History of England and Wales, iv. 1500–1640* (Cambridge, 1967), p. 817.

141 I owe this suggestion to Mr C.S.L. Davies.

142 I.S.W. Blanchard, 'Population change, enclosure and the early Tudor economy', *Economic History Review*, xxiii (1970), pp. 427–45. It has been argued that agricultural families in the primarily leadmining villages of the Mendips and Derbyshire had often temporarily alienated properties surplus to immediate requirements to the more prosperous miners but that population growth and inflation from the 1510s led to fewer alienations and thus reduced opportunities for non-landholders. (I. Blanchard, 'Industrial employment and the rural landmarket 1380–1520', in R.M. Smith, ed., *Land, Kinship and Life Cycle* (Cambridge, 1985 for 1984), pp. 244–9, 264–7). If similar relationships had existed but were being reduced in the Suffolk textile towns that might have made fiscal demands and any economic difficulties in the early 1520s the more burdensome.

143 C.A. Phythian-Adams, *Desolation of a city: Coventry and the urban crisis of the late middle ages* (Cambridge, 1979) pp. 52–60.

144 E.M. Carus-Wilson and O. Coleman, *England's export trade 1275–1547* (Oxford, 1963), p. 72.

145 *Ibid.*, pp. 115–16.

146 P.J. Bowden, *The wool trade in Tudor and Stuart England* (1962), p. 219; Clark, *English provincial society*, p. 21, is cautious, in writing of Kent, suggesting that the cloth trade was somewhat depressed but that there is no positive evidence of industrial crisis; cf. G.D. Ramsay, *The Wiltshire Woollen Industry* (2nd edn., 1965), p. 65; E.M. Carus-Wilson *Medieval Merchant Venturers* (2nd edn., 1967), pp. 5, 7–8.

6 The Amicable Grant and disturbances in the textile towns of Suffolk

The principal disturbances in 1525 occurred in the clothing towns of south-west Suffolk in and around Lavenham, Sudbury and Hadleigh and the Stour Valley. In early May large numbers gathered. Just how many is unknowable. The earl of Essex and Lord Fitzwalter reported an unlawful assembly on the borders of Suffolk adjoining Stansted, from where they were writing, of at least a thousand.[1]

Not oonly a greate parte of this shire [Suffolk] and of Essex but in lyke wyse Cambridgshire the Towne of Cambridge and the scolers there were all combyned to gathers vpon the rynging of bells to haue assembled to gethers and thought to haue gatherd the nom[bre] of xx^{ml} men within two dayes and twoo nightts

reported the dukes of Norfolk and Suffolk on 11 May. They said that they themselves had met at least 4,000 people near Lavenham.[2] That is the same number as Hall mentioned as rebelling from Lavenham, Sudbury, Hadleigh and other towns.[3] According to Griffith, over ten thousand assembled in and around Lavenham.[4] The only sources that list men by name supply 525 names from Lavenham and surrounding places who allegedly met at Lavenham market place on 4 May and Sudbury market place on 5 May.[5]

What these men, however many there were, intended to do is by no means clear. Evidently they wanted to halt the grant.

According to the indictment, implausibly identical for four gatherings, those assembled told the commissioners 'that no man shall pay no money to the kyng wherfor goo ye your wayes ye shall nott sitt here'.[6] They were persuading the inhabitants of Essex near Stansted not to agree to it: 'they do not only execute their malyciou[s] purpose theym selfes but also doth dayly procure and stere the inhabytauntes of these quarters to folowe the same'. Several honest persons who had granted were now in 'such fere of manassment of threttes of the bassest sortes of the comons' that they did not dare grant: 'for some haue showed . . . that if they make any grauntes that they shuld be hewen yn peces'. When some Essex men went to Sudbury in Suffolk, their market town, the Suffolk men 'doo there dayly procure theym to folowe theyr evyll dysposed purposes sayeng to theym that it were a good dede to hang theym that wolde make any suche graunt of any mony'.[7] According to the weaver in Griffith's chronicle, 'it was their intention to go to his grace the king to complain of the Cardinal on account of the taxes which he set men one day after another to demand of them'.[8] Henry feared that riotous persons would pass from Suffolk through Essex to London.[9] Beyond this, their intentions are not known: there are no articles of grievances.

The dukes of Norfolk and Suffolk, as we have seen, treated these assemblies as a military emergency and raised armed forces to deal with them. That alone shows that these disturbances were not a mere protest, not a ritual demonstration. Indeed Griffith noted that a majority of those involved were prepared to use force and to 'die like men in their quarrel'.[10] According to the chroniclers, Norfolk and Suffolk, strongly supported, went towards the rebels, met them and succeeded not only in dispersing them but in getting them to submit publicly. Griffith tells how some of the ten thousand and above assembled around Lavenham came to Norfolk and Suffolk, leaving their fellows in the town 'to watch unremittingly what the lords would do unto them' and in particular to set the bells in motion if the lords were seen to raise an alarm (presumably, that is, to prepare to use armed force). A long conference took place; the lords agreed to hear the people's grievances. A large number of commons then came and all spoke at once, 'like a flock of geese in corn'. Norfolk and

Suffolk told them to go away, to 'press' their heads together, to consider whether they would maintain their rebellion or whether they would submit to the king as breakers of his laws: if they chose to submit, they should choose a spokesman to show the reason for their armed assembly. Sixty were then sent by the rebels, coming in their nightshirts to show their obedience to the king and their repentance for causing a disturbance. The lords listened 'civilly' to their complaints and agreed 'to become their keepers and protectors against the king's ire for breaking the law'. Representatives of these sixty then returned to their fellows: a vigorous debate then took place whether they should submit or whether they should 'die like men in their quarrel with such as were daily despoiling them of whatever God sent them for the labour of their hands'. After 'a prolonged talk' the majority chose to resist. But confusion ensued when it was discovered that the clappers had been removed from the bells of the town. Those remaining in the field became anxious, fearing they had been betrayed, and consequently submitted, bareheaded and kneeling before the dukes, blaming their poverty for their offences. 'And everything was smoothed among the people in that part of the kingdom', Griffith tantalisingly concludes his account.[11] According to Hall, Norfolk came to the rebels, sent to them to know their purpose, and then met them. Their spokesman pleaded poverty, appealing to Norfolk to 'consider our necessitie'. After Norfolk offered to intercede with Henry for their pardon, the people of the country came to submit, in their shirts and with halters around their necks.[12] In their letters Norfolk and Suffolk give little indication of just how they induced the rebels to give up: they reported receiving the offenders of Lavenham and Brent Eleigh, in their shirts and kneeling for mercy, on 11 May, and they were intending to meet the inhabitants of Sudbury and Melford later.[13]

A recent discovery in the records of King's Bench by Diarmaid MacCulloch throws much new light on those involved in these disturbances.[14] This is a list of 525 men from nineteen places indicted for riot and unlawful assembly at a special commission of the peace held at Lavenham on 18 May. There were 170 from Lavenham, 48 from Waldingfield maior, 43 from Long Melford, 40 from Brent Eleigh, 33 from

Brettenham, 29 from Waldingfield parva, 26 from Monks Eleigh, 25 from Cockfield, 24 from Sudbury, 18 from Thorpe Morieux, 16 from Acton and from Preston. Many of those accused were textile workers. There were 65 weavers from Lavenham, 27 from the two Waldingfields, 16 from Melford. There were 23 fullers from Lavenham, nine from Monks Eleigh. There were eight dyers from Lavenham. There were ten shearmen from the two Waldingfields, nine from Lavenham, But if textile workers were prominent, it was not just a revolt by them. The largest single occupational group was that of labourer (161 men). There were tailors, butchers, shoemakers, smiths; there were five bakers, five carpenters, five wheelwrights, three cobblers, three coopers, three cordwainers, three tanners, three tallowchandlers, two carvers, two fletchers, two freemasons, two thatchers, two turners and so on. Outside Lavenham, husbandmen were involved: nine from Brettenham, seven from Cockfield, six from Preston, five from Brent Eleigh, five from Alpheton. Can one speak of a revolt of a whole community? In some places the rate at which the inhabitants participated in the troubles is astonishingly high. The list of those indicted in 1525 can be compared with those listed in the subsidy returns of 1524. Of the 1,178 named in the subsidy returns for the nineteen places from which those accused in 1525 came, some 295 (25%) were indicted in 1525. The proportion in certain places was even higher. Of the 182 named in the 1524 subsidy list for Lavenham, 90 (50%) were indicted in 1525; of the 23 in Brettenham, 15 (62%) were indicted; of the 27 in Brent Eleigh, 18 (66%) were indicted. Of course the subsidy returns of 1524 do not record the whole population: those regarded as too poor to pay the subsidy were not usually listed. There are many indicted in 1525 whose names do not appear in the subsidy lists. Some of this would reflect migration. But the vast bulk of those not recorded in the subsidy lists must have been people too poor to pay the subsidy. Eighty of those indicted from Lavenham were not in the subsidy list, eighteen from Brent Eleigh, fourteen from Brettenham. There is no sure way of knowing the total population of these places. But however one estimates the numbers of those excluded from the subsidy (and these figures suggest that a good many were excluded) it does seem very likely that a high proportion of the inhabitants of these places, and especially of Lavenham, took part in the troubles. Should these be seen as a revolt of the poor? 226 of those indicted were not recorded in the subsidy lists: if, as is likely, they were too poor to pay, then this is useful evidence for such an interpretation. Further, the participation rates of those assessed at £1 in the 1524 subsidy (the lowest value at which people were to be assessed) were high. In Lavenham, of 98 in the subsidy list at £1, 61 (or 61%) were indicted in 1525; in Brettenham, of ten, eight (80%) were indicted; in Brent Eleigh, of twelve, nine (75%) were indicted; in Cockfield, of twenty, nine (45%) were indicted, in Thorpe Morieux, of seventeen, seven (40%) were indicted; in Milden, Monks Eleigh, Preston and the Waldingfields, the proportion was around 25–30%. In all the nineteen places from which those indicted in 1525 came, there were 614 assessed at £1 in 1524: of these 164 were indicted in 1525. Of the total of 177 assessed at between £1 and £2, 45 were indicted; of the 117 assessed at between £2 and £5, 30 were indicted; of the 252 assessed at £5 and upwards, 35 were indicted. Clearly the bulk of those accused were poor: 390 out of the total of 525 indicted were either not assessed at all in 1524 (presumably because of poverty) or assessed at £1. Something like a quarter of those assessed at £5 or under in 1524 were indicted in 1525. Locally the proportions could be much higher. But only in a few places was a majority of any group categorised by subsidy assessments involved.

Figures of this sort cannot prove whether or not the troubles were authentically popular. On the face of it, the 'poor' were significantly involved, especially in Lavenham and neighbouring clothworking places. The large numbers of those worth £1 or (presumably) less that were indicted strengthen the case for seeing the revolt as inspired not so much by the Amicable Grant itself but by fears of the economic dislocation it would create, and especially by fears of unemployment which would hit the poor harder than a single payment to the king. Yet if it is true that few men worth over £5 were indicted, nevertheless, some were, especially in the more agricultural places outside Lavenham where a wider cross-section of society, including some husbandmen, took part, and in any case indictments could be socially selective, sparing gentry and clothiers. Nothing from these statistics can prove which social group was most prominent in the rising, though they do show that it was not a revolt of just the most marginal. Nor can anything from these figures conclusively dispose of the possibility that the troubles were stirred from above.

Here the question that must be asked is what was the role of the clothiers? They were vitally important in the cloth industry. They bought raw wool, recruited and paid various craftspeople — weavers, spinners, fullers — and organised the sale and despatch of finished cloth.[15] The greatest of them was Thomas Spring III of Lavenham who had died in 1523. How heavily did the loans, taxes and grants demanded in these years bear upon them? Was Skelton right that

> Good Sprynge of La[ve]n[h]am
> Muste counte what became
> Of his clothe makynge
> He is at suche takynge
> Though his purs wax dull
> He must tax for his wull . . .
>
> In the spyght of his tethe
> He must pay agayn
> A thousande or twayne
> Of golde in store
> And yet he payde before
> An hundred pounde and more
> Whiche pyncheth him sore!
> My lordis grace [Wolsey] wyll brynge
> Downe this hye sprynge;
> And brynge it so lowe
> It shall nat ever flowe.[16]

If this was splendidly exaggerated, it does nonetheless seem quite possible that clothiers may have faced difficulties at a time of renewed fiscality and low wool prices. In 1525, according to Hall, the duke of Suffolk had sat in the county of Suffolk and 'by gentle handling, he caused the riche Clothiers to assent and graunt to geue the sixt parte', that is they agreed to pay the Amicable Grant in full. But they then returned home, called together their spinners, carders, fullers, weavers and other artificers, 'whiche were wont to be set a woorke and haue their liuynges by cloth makyng', and told them that 'our

goodes be taken from vs' and that they were now unable to set
them to work. It was then that women wept, young folks cried,
while 'men that had no woorke began to rage, and assemble
theimselfes in compaignies', railing against Suffolk and
threatening him and Wolsey with death.[17] Their spokesman
later explained to the duke of Norfolk that the rebels

liue not of ourselfes, but . . . by the substanciall occupiers of this
countrey . . . if they by whom we liue, be brought in that case that they of
their litle, cannot helpe vs to earne our liuyng, then must we perishe and dye
miserably. . . . the cloth makers haue put all these people, and a farre greater
nomber [than were assembled there] from worke.[18]

Norfolk and Suffolk reported on 11 May that as the commons
submitted, they said they had offended 'oonly for lacke of work
soo that they knewe not howe to gett theire lyvinges'.[19] Earlier
the duke of Norfolk had reported the warnings of the authorities
of Norwich that

the living of theim of the citie was moste by worsted and stamen making
whiche was wrought by thandes of many a thousand and muste bee paid
euery weke and if they shuld delyuer out all theire redy money they could not
have the said worsted and stamen made, and consequently the Towne shuld
fall to extreme ruyne and the country in lyke wyse for lack of occupacion.[20]

Were the refusals and troubles of the Amicable Grant provoked
by the unemployment, or by the fears of unemployment,
especially of textile workers?

And what of the role of the clothiers? Did they provoke
rebellion quite unwittingly as they passed on the consequences
of their acceptance of royal demands? Or was there more
conscious design in their actions: did they hope that popular
disorders might produce a reduction or a cancellation of such
demands? The evidence for 1525 permits no deductions.
Thomas Spring III's son, John, and his son-in-law, Thomas
Jermyn, were sent by the dukes of Norfolk and Suffolk to
induce the commons to submit; Hall noted that 'in especiall one
Master Iermyn, toke muche pain in ridyng and goyng betwene
the lordes and commons'.[21] But they acted perhaps more as
local gentry than as men with any continuing interest as
clothiers.

Some light may be thrown on these questions by evidence of

fears of disorders in 1528. It is clear that clothiers could and did lay men off in poor economic circumstances. Sir Henry Guildford wrote from Leeds, Kent, that the clothiers complained that they made so few sales that 'they be not able to kepe so many on worke as they haue donne in tymes past. And yf they be drivin be necessite to leve their occupacion a greate compain shalbe set to ydelnes'.[22] Humfrey Monmouth, the London draper arrested on suspicion of heresy, complained how since his arrest he had utterly lost his name and credit. He had used to buy cloths in Suffolk, paying for them weekly. If the clothiers from whom he had bought could no longer get money from him, they would not be able to set the poor folks to work. Other merchants would not buy those cloths he had taken before.[23] In March the duke of Norfolk summoned forty of the most substantial clothers of the area around Stoke-by-Nayland, and 'with the best wordes I could vse perswaded them to contynew the settyng of their workfolkes on werk' and to take back that day those servants they had dismissed. If he had not quashed rumours of the arrests of English merchants in Flanders, he would have had 200 or 300 women sueing him to make the clothiers set them, their husbands and their children to work as they were wont to do. He advised Wolsey to get the London merchants not to allow so many cloths to remain unsold in Blackwell Hall, the London exchange for cloths from East Anglia.[24] In May he warned Wolsey that divers substantial clothiers had been to see him 'makyng lamentable complaynt' that they could find no buyers for their cloths in London and that unless some solution were found they would be unable to keep their workfolks in work for more than a fortnight or three weeks.[25]

The circumstances of 1528 were not the same as those of 1525. In 1528 a diplomatic and trading row between England and the emperor was harming the export of English cloth to the Netherlands. The harvest of 1527 had been one of the poorest of the century: breadcorn had been in desperately short supply in the winter of 1527–8, 'the worst and most dangerous in living memory'.[26] But what does emerge relevantly from these letters of 1528 is the fragility and vulnerability of employment in the cloth industry. A sudden shock — such as the financial demand of 1525 — could have a swift and severe impact. What is even more significant is the belief voiced in 1528 that clothiers could provoke disorders. In March Lord Sandys was informed by the king that

certein light persones clothiers servantes and other haue assembled theymselffes in an vnlaufull nombr aboutes Westbury. Affermyng that by reason their meisters have not payment of such somes as be owing vnto theym for their cloths in London and other places they be expelled from their werke having no meane to get their lyving

and a few days later he was ordered by the king to be vigilant

that noo clothmekre opon payn of his high displeasor and indignacion shall discharge eny artificer which heretofore they haue put in occupacion aboutes the drepyng of their cloths by reason whereof eny vnlaufull assemble might arrise to the violation of the peace or provocation of eny other light persons to doo the semblable.[27]

In early April the earl of Essex sent on a letter in which a Joseph Boswell of Colchester wrote to 'good man Sammys' that they could not sell cloth here even at half the cost price and that 'therefor we be fayne to lene vp for in feith we haue scant money ynough for to pay the spinners that be abrode when they come home with the work'. Most significantly, he then added the remark that 'the marchantes sayth that they wyll not buy a cloth *without that we can cause the comyne to arise for to complayne to the kyng and show hyme how they be not halff set a wourke*'.[28] Boswell, a clothmaker, was examined by the bailiffs of Colchester and reiterated what he had written. He had written it because he owed Sames money and wanted him to give him longer in which to pay. When recently in London, he had met, in Colchester Hall within Blackwell Hall, one John Tyndall, a London merchant, to whom he had offered his cloths. Tyndall told him he would not be able to re-sell them; and when Boswell asked him what the remedy was, Tyndall, significantly, said that '*he coude tell of noune, except we coode cause the comons to arise and complayne to the kynges grace and schewe hym how the people be not halff set awourke*'.[29] The case must remain circumstantial, but if the assemblies of 1525 are to be seen as stirred up from above, the clothiers of southern Suffolk seem the most plausible instigators.

And yet the evidence of 'class conflict' in 1525 does put into doubt such a supposition. How much resentment was there of the rich by the commons? How far did the authorities and the clothiers fear the multitude? Before looking at East Anglia, we must briefly consider the evidence from other areas. In London according to Hall the mayor refused to accede to Wolsey's demand for a benevolence on 8 May, saying that 'if I should entre into any graunt it might fortune me to cost me my life'. When on the following day common council declared that every man should go to Wolsey and grant privily what he would, the citizens 'in a furie' wanted two mercers and a merchant tailor who was also a serjeant at arms expelled from the council. How far did 'class hatred' lie behind such threats? Certainly Hall's account of the Amicable Grant in London suggests divisions between mayor and aldermen and common council on the one hand and the commons on the other.[30] Hall also noted how in Kent, Lord Cobham sent one John Skudder, who 'answered hym clubbishly', to the Tower and how people 'muttered and grudged the Lorde Cobham' and 'in this grudge . . . euill entreated Sir Thomas Bullein'.[31] In early May the Kentish commissioners saw it as 'hard' 'to enduce a wilful and indiscrete multitude to any reason, which will folowe their wittes and no wisedome ne yet good counsell'. Warham thought it a waste of time to 'practise' with those worth less than £20: 'for suche pouer people that be of litle substaunce and have but litle to loose carith litle what busynes they make and wolbe more ready to do myscheife then they that hath somewhat'.[32] Similarly he and his fellow commissioners feared that

such persons of whome the more parte hath but litle substaunce be more apte to make more busynes then men of greatter substaunce woll. And in asmoch as the said persons of small substaunce be farr moo in nomember than the other sorteis bee, which in discrete multitude it shalbe verye harde to ordre, bicause multitudes commonly be more ruled after thaire own selfe wilfulnes than after good reason or discretion, and some woll fall into fumes and so fallen woll not be ruled by other persons nether can nor woll well rule or ordre thaymselues.[33]

In mid-May Warham wrote of 'an indiscrete and inordinate multitude of theym which at euery light fleeyng tale be inclined and kendled to il imaginations, inuentions, and ill attemptates rather than to good'. Some honest and substantial men who

had granted were thinking of leaving the country for a while 'for
fere of ill disposed people'.[34] Hall spoke of the abandonment of
the grant as not ending the 'inwarde grudge and hatered, that
the commons bare to the Cardinall, and *to all gentlemen,* whiche
vehemently set furth that commission and demaunde'.[35] How
far do these comments show popular resentment of those who
had granted or who were administering the grant, how far do
they reveal popular hostility, or fears of popular hostility,
against the upper orders in general?

In East Anglia Hall tells us that 'the people railed openly on
the Duke of Suffolk and Sir Robert Drurie, and threatened
them with death'. Suffolk's men offered to defend him from
perils but would not fight against their neighbours.[36] Ellis
Griffith suggests the possibility of some division between
clothiers and their workfolk when he describes how an
unnamed rich man in Lavenham had removed the clappers
from the bells, which made it impossible for the rebels to
mobilise their forces at a crucial point in the troubles, a failure
which led directly to the submission of the rebels. Griffith's
rebels were divided amongst themselves, as we have seen,
between those prepared to fight and those willing to submit,
and Griffith puts no words of 'class conflict' into the mouth of
their spokesmen.[37] Hall, however, does. John Green described
how the clothiers provided employment but went on 'and yet
they geue vs so litle wages for our workmanship, that scarcely
we be able to liue, and thus in penurie we passe the tyme, we
our wifes and children'.[38] The commissioners were certainly
fearful of popular disturbances. This might be because they
were stirring up, or making the most of, the troubles for their
own ends, and so needed to exaggerate the level of violence, but
this is not an interpretation that was found persuasive above. It
does seem rather that their worries were sincere and, indeed,
justified. No doubt most popular criticism of the upper classes
in 1525 was directed at gentlemen and clothiers not because of
their privileges as such, but because of their part, whether as
commissioners, or as early grantors, in furthering the Amicable
Grant, but there was at least an undertow of deeper
resentment. There was a danger that 'political' and 'social'
grievances could become fused, that Henry and Wolsey, the
nobles and churchmen who were directing the demand, and the

lesser commissioners who were administering it locally, could come to be seen as a single system of oppression.[39] Perhaps commissioners may have remembered the fate of the fourth earl of Northumberland, murdered by the commons while collecting taxation in Yorkshire in 1489.

Were the government and commissioners influenced by news of contemporary rebellions in Germany? Pace wrote of these from Venice on 7 April, Fitzwilliam and Robert Wingfield from the Low Countries on 5, 8, 9, 13, 20, 22 May. Wolsey, at least, must have known of these insurrections by mid-May.[40] Hall offers a brief paragraph about the German troubles immediately after his account of the Amicable Grant, interestingly using the linking phrase 'in this trobelous season'.[41] But there is nothing to allow a definite connection between commissioners' fears and the German rebellions.

Was the extreme humiliation and submission that the dukes of Norfolk and Suffolk imposed on the rebels an expression of their reaction to the temporary collapse of order and social discipline? The inhabitants of Lavenham and Brent Eleigh came before the dukes in their shirts and kneeling 'with pitious crying for mercy'.[42] This was a ceremony emphasising their subordination and re-creating publicly the authority of the dukes as rulers of that country and as natural mediators between the inhabitants and the king (though what the dukes offered to obtain was royal clemency rather than any change of policy). If this sketch of the fears of the ruling class is correct, it raises difficulties about any overall view of the Suffolk troubles as a demonstration in which the clothiers responded to new financial demands by stirring up their workfolks to protest in large assemblies which they then controlled and helped to pacify, and which were followed by submission to the dukes who would report events to the king, who would then cancel the demands. This plays down the real fears of the commissioners, the threats of force, the severity of repression. There is no hint of any conspiracy between clothiers and their workers, there was no interrogation or punishment of clothiers. John Spring seems to have been doing what he could to quiet the rebels. It was not just clothiers, after all, who were laying off men because of the Amicable Grant. John Green, the rebels' spokesman, told the duke of Norfolk that 'the husbande men haue put away their

seruauntes, and geuen vp houshold, they say, the kyng asketh
so much, that thei be not able to do as thei haue done before this
tyme'.[43] In the last analysis, Warham's assessment was the
most plausible: those with least to lose were the most likely to
protest vigorously and spontaneously. Much of the evidence is
of course more difficult to interpret than a first glance suggests,
but it seems unnecessary to argue that the revolt of the Suffolk
textile workers and agricultural labourers (and even yeomen)
in 1525 was anything other than a spontaneous and
understandable reaction to the unemployment, or fear of
unemployment, arising from the impact, or feared impact, on
their local economy of the Amicable Grant.

Notes

1 PRO SP1/34/fos. 192–3 (*LP*, IV, i 1321).
2 B.L. Cotton MS, Cleopatra F vi fos. 325, 326 (Ellis, *Original Letters*, 3rd series, ii. 3–6; *LP*, IV, i 1323).
3 Hall, *Chronicle*, p. 699.
4 *HMC, Wales*, i. p. ii.
5 PRO KB 9/497/ 7,8,9, cited by R.L. Woods, 'Individuals in the rioting crowd', pp. 1–24 (I owe this reference to Professor C.S.R. Russell). Woods' reconstruction of the rebels' itinerary (pp. 6, 13–15) is speculative and is not borne out by the chroniclers' evidence.
6 KB 9/497/ 6–9 cited by Woods, *loc. cit.*
7 PRO SP1/34/fos. 192–92ᵛ (*LP*, IV i 1321).
8 *HMC, Wales*, i. p. iv.
9 *HMC, 3rd report, appendix, Bath*, p. 202.
10 *HMC, Wales*, i. pp. iii–iv.
11 *Ibid.*
12 Hall, *Chronicle*, p. 700.
13 B.L. Cotton MS, Cleopatra F vi fo. 325–325ᵛ (Ellis, *Original Letters*, 3rd series, ii. 3, 5; *LP*, IV, i 1323); cf. PRO SP1/34/fo. 196 (*LP*, IV, i 1329).
14 PRO KB 29/157 mm. 5–6. (I am very grateful to Dr D.N.J. MacCulloch not only for drawing my attention to this reference in the controlment rolls but also for lending me his index cards correlating those indicted in 1525 with the subsidy return of 1524. Some of the calculations that follow are based on my own counts using the latter.) A similar list in the ancient indictments (PRO KB 9/497/6–9) was discovered independently by R.L. Woods, 'Individuals in the rioting crowd'. My discussion takes these lists at face value, but it is worth asking just how and by whom those indicted were chosen from the larger populations of these towns and villages: it is remarkable that so large and so specific a list could be compiled at all. Is it safe to assume that all, or only, those named were involved in the insurrection? Were no women involved?

15 D. Dymond and A. Betterton, *Lavenham: 700 years of textile making* (Woolbridge, 1982), pp. 12–13.

16 J. Scattergood, ed., *John Skelton: the complete poems* (1983), pp. 302–3 lines 933–52.

17 Hall, *Chronicle*, p. 699.

18 *Ibid.*, p. 700.

19 B.L. Cotton MS, Cleopatra F vi fo. 325 (Ellis, *Original Letters*, 3rd series, ii. 3–4; *LP*, IV, i 1323).

20 B.L. Cotton MS, Cleopatra F vi fo. 337 (Ellis, *Original Letters*, 3rd series, i. 379; *LP*, IV, i 1235).

21 PRO SP1/34/fo. 209 (*LP*, IV, 1343); Hall, *Chronicle*, p. 700.

22 PRO SP1/48/fo. 24 (*LP*, IV, ii 4276).

23 *LP*, IV, ii 4282.

24 PRO SP1/47/fos. 59–60, 83ᵛ (*LP*, IV, ii 4012, 4044).

25 PRO SP1/48/fo. 1 (*LP*, IV, ii 4239).

26 D. Dymond, 'The famine of 1527 in Essex', *Local Population Studies*, xxvi (1981), pp. 29–40 at pp. 29, 32–3.

27 PRO SP1/47/fos. 82, 154 (*LP*, IV, ii 4043, 4058). The *LP* reading of the latter, 'so as to cause unlawful assemblies', is too free.

28 PRO SP1/47/fo. 152 (*LP*, IV, i 4129 (i) and (ii)). My italics.

29 PRO SP1/47/fos. 162–3 (*LP*, IV, ii 4145 (i) and (ii)). My italics. Most probably 'more like exasperation than rebellion' (Kennedy, thesis cit., pp. 220–1), but can one be certain?

30 Hall, *Chronicle*, pp. 698–9.

31 *Ibid.*, p. 699.

32 B.L. Cotton MS, Cleopatra F vi fo. 349 (Ellis, *Original Letters*, 3rd series, i. 366; *LP*, IV, i 1266).

33 PRO SP1/34/fo. 173 (not in *LP*, IV, i 1306). In 1528 Warham noted that 'comonly in a multitude the more parte lack both wytt and discretion and yet the same more parte woll take vpon theym to rule the wyser' (PRO SP1/47/fo. 209 (*LP*, IV ii 4188).

34 B.L. Cotton MS, Cleopatra F vi fo. 341–41ᵛ (Ellis, *Original Letters*, 3rd series, ii. 9–10; *LP*, IV, i 1332).

35 Hall, *Chronicle*, p. 702. My italics. I owe this point to my former undergraduate Mr J. Mears.

36 *Ibid.*, pp. 699–700.

37 *HMC, Wales*, i. pp. iii–iv.

38 Hall, *Chronicle*, p. 700.

39 Cf. suggestive comments, in a different context, of C.C. Dyer, 'The social and economic background to the rural revolt of 1381', in R.H. Hilton and T.H. Aston, eds., *The English Rising of 1381* (Cambridge, 1984), pp. 38–9.

40 *LP*, IV, i 1251, 1312, 1320, 1322, 1333, 1346, 1350.

41 Hall, *Chronicle*, p. 702; cf. A.J. Fletcher, *Tudor Rebellions* (3rd edn., 1983), p. 15.

42 B.L. Cotton MS, Cleopatra F vi fo. 325 (Ellis, *Original Letters*, 3rd series, ii. 3; *LP*, IV, i 1323).

43 Hall, *Chronicle*, p. 700.

7 Constitutional objections, arbitrary methods, despotic ambitions

The commons of the Suffolk clothing towns protested because the Amicable Grant was putting them out of work; most of those who refused the commissioners' demands did so because, despite their good will, they were too poor to agree to pay. But how far was there also resistance and refusal because the Amicable Grant was unconstitutional, a tax in all but name, and a tax unsanctioned by parliament? How brutal were the methods used by the crown and its agents in 1525? And how far did the attempt to levy an Amicable Grant reveal despotic intentions on the part of the government?

Hall's *Chronicle* provides the strongest evidence for seeing the Amicable Grant in constitutional terms. 'All the people curssed the cardinal and his coadherentes', he wrote, 'as subuersor of the lawes and libertie of Englande. For thei saied, if men should geue their goodes by a commission, then wer it worse then the taxes of Fraunce, and so England should be bond and not free'.[1] When commissioners were sent out into the shires, the demand was refused with complaints that 'they that sent furthe suche commissioners were subuerters of the lawe, and worthy to be punished as traytors'.[2] The clergy raised constitutional objections.

In euery assembly the priestes answered, that thei would pay nothyng, except it were graunted by conuocacion, otherwise not: for thei saied, that neuer kyng of England did aske any mannes goodes, but by an ordre of the lawe, and this commission is not by the ordre of the lawe: wherefore they saied, that the Cardinall and all the doers thereof were enemies to the kyng, and to the common wealthe.[3]

150

In London, Hall described the constitutional objections to the request for the benevolence that replaced the Amicable Grant. A city councillor told Wolsey that by the law no benevolence might be asked nor men examined individually by a commissioner as these practices were prohibited by an act of parliament made in the first year of the reign of Richard III. Wolsey quashed this by asking how the acts of so evil a usurper and murderer of his nephews could be good; the councillor replied 'although he did euill, yet in his tyme wer many good actes made not by hym onely, but by the consent of the body of the whole realme, whiche is the parliament'. The matter was not resolved before the benevolence was abandoned.[4] In Hall's account, Henry and Wolsey both denied that what they were doing was unlawful. Henry asserted that it had never been his intention to ask anything of his commons that might be 'to the breche of his lawes'.[5] Wolsey described how when it had been discussed how to make the king rich, 'the Kynges Counsaill, and especially the Iudges saied, he might lawfully demaunde any some by commission . . . and the spirituall men saie that it standeth with Goddes lawe, for Ioseph caused the kyng of Egipte to take the fifth parte of euery mannes goodes'.[6] The point here is not that Henry's and Wolsey's claims may have been specious but that Hall presents them as seeking to justify their actions in constitutional terms. The framework that supports Hall's account of the Amicable Grant is constitutional. For Hall, the Amicable Grant was regarded as an illegal, extra-parliamentary demand which, if allowed, would have led to government by commission and the subversion of English liberty. Herbert's later *Life and Raigne of Henry VIII* draws heavily on Hall and emphasises this aspect. The people took the demand so ill 'that it was like to have grown to a Rebellion: alledging, first, that these commissions were against the law'.[7] According to some notes made for but not used by Herbert, the people declared that 'they will not grant any thing by letters missives, but only by Act of Parliament'.[8] But Herbert was not a contemporary. Moreover Hall was writing years after these events, and however interesting his constitutional framework is, it must be treated with caution. What is striking is how little support for such an interpretation can be found in any other sources. One George Cob told William Wodwall of Rugby that 'he hade no justyes to paye ys money',[9] but it is by no means sure that this refers to the Amicable Grant. Only the clergy reported by Warham from Kent in mid-April raised, or hinted at, constitutional objections. They would, they claimed, be utterly destitute

if the kynges grace shuld now and also in tyme to come thus by his graces letters missives, privy seales, or other weys herafter require aide of the spiritualtie as often tymes as it shal please his grace so to doo besides the grauntes of convocations to which they knowlege theymselues bound.

They recognised that they had an obligation to accept grants voted by convocation; they did not feel obliged, though they refrained from saying so directly, to other demands by the crown.[10] But elsewhere in Warham's letters, or in the letters sent by the dukes of Norfolk and Suffolk, there is no sign of any constitutional objections. Even the clergy of Kent seem to have been protesting not so much on a point of principle but because they feared that repeated royal demands would reduce them to destitution. Where the Amicable Grant was refused or resisted, it was overwhelmingly on the grounds of poverty and inability to pay. The difficulty in concluding from this that constitutional issues were not paramount is not just that it is unwise to argue too confidently from silence but more importantly that, as we have seen, debates over royal financial demands were conducted in a different language, that of necessity and poverty. Dr G.L. Harriss has shown how the doctrine of necessity gave the crown the right to ask for aid from subjects in an emergency; those subjects could not refuse assistance outright but might plead that despite their good will, they were unable to pay.[11] It would therefore be wrong to look for constitutional objections to the Amicable Grant. The government's purpose was urgent and financial, not constitutional and fundamental. There is nothing to suggest that a parliament was not summoned because parliaments were thought to be troublesome, or that the Amicable Grant was seen by the government as a way of obtaining what a parliament had refused. On the contrary, the parliament of 1523 had voted taxation at high rates. Nor was the future summons of a parliament being made conditional on the payment of the Amicable Grant. More important is that there simply would not have been enough time to summon parliament and await the collection of a parliamentary tax: moreover many of those who would have been involved in that would also have been required for any invasion of France. Nor did the government persist in its demands once opposition grew, the crucial difference between the Amicable Grant and Charles I's forced loan of 1626.[12] But that is not to claim that what the government was doing was free from constitutional implications, although that leaves open the question of contemporary awareness of them. What is unknowable, of course, is how far discussion of a demand in these terms of necessity and poverty cloaked real constitutional concerns that it was impolitic and perhaps unnecessary to express: in this light, Hall's emphasis on law (in the absence of any reason why he should have invented or exaggerated)[13] is the more remarkable.

How despotic were the methods used to secure the Amicable Grant? That doctrine of necessity carried the corollary that royal demands should not be imposed by force but should be consented to. For this reason those who were required to pay in 1525 were asked first to acquiesce in the grant: their acquiescence made the grant just.[14] Of course the process of obtaining consent was meant to be merely formal, but the opportunity given for refusal was real and seized upon by many. How far were men bullied into agreement? There was nothing unusual about the use of noblemen and prelates to enforce this type of demand. They were certainly vigorous. Warham used 'long communications and the best perswasions' to get those who were to serve as county commissioners under him to acquiesce.[15] He described how he handled refusers sent by them 'with smothe wordes and rough'.[16] He urged Wolsey to take exemplary action against lay refusers sent up to him or to the king.[17] He threatened those whom he lectured in mid-April: banding together might cost them their lives; the king would take their unkindness heavily; going before the council would cost them as much in expenses as making the requested contribution; they risked confiscation of their goods if their pleas of poverty were later discovered to be unfounded.[18] Lord Cobham handled men 'roughly' in Kent.[19] The duke of Norfolk had so entreated two hundred refusers sent to him 'that not oon hathe said nay'. What did he say to them?[20] How far did he do more than just jolly along the citizens of Norwich when he got them to make a fresh start at the end of April?[21] Bishop West of Ely wrote how after meeting with some reluctance to grant, he had eventually succeeded, 'eftsones persuadyng them by all meanes and wayes possible to condiscend to the kinges pleasor'. 'And so at lengith with great labor busynes and goode polecye vsed bothe with fayer wordes and some rowgh handelyng of oon or twayn whiche I founde more obstinate in this behalve than any other I browght them to graunt the same, makyng muche dollowr and lamentacyon'. He handled some fifty refusers 'in suche goode maner that after som good persuasyons to them made I browght them to a goode poynte'.[22] The earl of Essex and Lord Fitzwalter 'practysed' with certain townships 'accordyng vnto our Instruccyons and with moche difficulty and persuasyons brought the most parte to condiscend and graunt'.[23] The marquess of Dorset had used 'good meanes and persuasions' in Warwickshire.[24] The most vivid impression of despotic methods comes from Hall's account of Wolsey's practising of the demands in London, but this must read in the context of Hall's dislike of Wolsey and of his stress on the constitutional issues raised by the Amicable Grant. Wolsey's announcement of the demand reduced the mayor and aldermen to silent astonishment. He threatened them, 'beware and resist not, nor ruffill not in this case, for it maie fortune to cost some their heddes'. Then, every day for a fortnight, Wolsey sent for a certain number of commoners, to persuade them to grant: some replied in such a way 'that they were sent to ward'. Meanwhile Wolsey also severely criticised Lord Lisle for writing a letter from Reading, Berkshire, reporting the offer of the inhabitants to pay one-twelfth instead of one-sixth: 'it should cost the Lord Lisle his hedde, and his landes should be solde to paie the kyng the values, that by him and you folishe commissioners [he was talking to one of them, Sir Richard Weston] he had lost, and all your liues at the kynges will'.[25] Yet if there is undoubtedly a despotic flavour about these actions reported by commissioners and described by Hall, in the last resort the strength of the refusals suggests that many felt not at all intimidated. Some of those who agreed to grant, moreover, may have had no intention of paying when the time came, as the dukes of Norfolk and Suffolk were to suspect.[26] As in the fourteenth century, so in 1525, complaints and refusals were a mark not so much of oppression but of the many opportunities for resistance in a by no means unfree society.[27]

The demand for an Amicable Grant failed. In the end it proved impossible for the crown to raise further large sums of money from its subjects. Resistance did not come from the council: the duke of Norfolk, the earl of Shrewsbury, Sir Richard Wingfield, Thomas More and the bishop of London, all present on 10 March, must have approved the proposal.[28] The judges raised no objections. The nobility and higher clergy did not oppose the demand: indeed the dukes of Norfolk and Suffolk, the marquess of Dorset, the earls of Essex and Oxford, Lords Cobham and Fitzwalter, the archbishop of Canterbury and the bishops of Ely and Lincoln, all of whom were commissioners, certainly did not protest against it openly and almost certainly (as has been argued above) were not secretly undermining it, but were rather serving the crown loyally and skilfully in attempting to implement a difficult command. Thus far the Amicable Grant vividly illustrates the strength and confidence of the government: it could rely on its greater subjects to foster its purposes in the localities and it was confident enough to risk exposing them by association to popular criticism of royal policy. At the level immediately below, those men who were to act as commissioners within counties did require some persuasion to acquiesce but ultimately they did. There was disquiet among the leading citizens of Norwich but they were nonetheless willing to administer the grant. The mayor and aldermen of London seemed to have stalled in April but in early May they were actively trying to raise a benevolence.[29] It was those who were not commissioners but who were worth £20 upwards that produced difficulties and, at least in Kent, lasting but peaceful refusals, and possibly a kind of passive resistance by boycotting local markets. It is therefore not quite accurate to speak of a breakdown between the crown and the tax-paying class: there was rather a split within that class. The dukes of Norfolk and Suffolk persuaded their counties of Norfolk and Suffolk to grant; Wolsey claimed that Middlesex and adjoining shires had agreed to grant.[30] But more generally reluctance and refusal abounded: in London, in Kent, at Reading, in Warwickshire, among the clergy, and no doubt in many other counties for which no evidence survives.[31] This resistance persuaded the government to reduce its demands, though not uniformly, in late April and early May. And it was then the continuing difficulties in London and Kent and especially the more forceful assembly of the commons of the textile towns of southern Suffolk and adjacent counties, fearful of the unemployment that the demand would produce, that led to such disturbances, and fears of greater troubles, that finally persuaded Henry and Wolsey to abandon the grant. That was a mark of the weakness of Tudor government — but also of its flexibility: fiscal oppression was not driven too hard.

The demand failed because it followed so hard on the exactions of previous years, possibly making an especially heavy impact in Suffolk. It failed because it was a sudden response to the new military opportunities created by the battle of Pavia rather than a carefully considered scheme to extract money without parliamentary sanction and so to foster royal power. It failed because royal foreign policy had become so conditional, so unsuccessful in achieving triumphs, that it was impossible to mount a convincing campaign of propaganda. Its main consequences were twofold. First, the government did not dare make further recourse to general financial demands on the scale of the mid-1510s and early 1520s for well over a decade. In the early 1540s benevolences and loans did resume, alongside parliamentary taxes, but with crucial differences. The loan of 1542 was restricted to the better off, that of 1544 to higher clergy and noblemen. The more general benevolence of 1545 was levied during war rather than before it, and its rates, as shown by the yield of £71,000, were much more comparable to those of a subsidy than to the remarkably high rates of the loan of 1522–3 or the Amicable Grant.[32] The protests of 1525 significantly reduced the fiscal possibilities of Henrician government. Secondly, the immediate lack of money in 1525 reinforced growing mistrust of Charles V and led to peace with France, settled by the Treaty of the More in August 1525, and a longer period in which France was seen as England's ally. The failure of the Amicable Grant thus had profound and lasting consequences. And yet, in the scale of the demand, and in the accompanying vision of an English king conquering and partitioning France, the Amicable Grant furnishes a study of Tudor government not only at its least effective but also at its most ambitious.

Notes

1 Hall, *Chronicle*, p. 696.
2 *Ibid.*, p. 697.
3 *Ibid.*, p. 696.
4 *Ibid.*, pp. 698, 701.
5 *Ibid.*, p. 700.
6 *Ibid.*
7 E. Herbert, *The Life and Raigne of Henry VIII* (1649), p. 173.
8 Bodleian Library, MS Jesus c. 74 (*LP*, IV, i 1318).
9 *LP*, IV, i 1567.
10 B.L. Cotton MS, Titus B i fo. 273 (*LP*, IV, i 1267). There is nothing to give firmer support to the contention that 'county opinion viewed the loan [*sic*] as a fiscal device to bypass parliament as the established source of extraordinary revenue' (Clark, *English provincial society*, p. 21).
11 Harriss, 'Aids, loans and benevolences', *loc. cit.*, and other references above, p. 130 n. 9.
12 I have benefited here from reflecting on R.P. Cust, 'The forced loan and English politics, 1626–8', University of London Ph.D. thesis, 1984, and 'Charles I, the privy council and the forced loan', *Journal of British Studies*, xxiv (1985), pp. 208–35.
13 I owe this suggestion to Mrs J. Loach.
14 Harriss, 'Aids, loans and benevolences', pp. 6–7.
15 B.L. Cotton MS, Cleopatra F vi fo. 339 (Ellis, *Original Letters*, 3rd series, i. p. 369; *LP*, IV, 1243).
16 B.L. Cotton MS, Cleopatra F vi fo. 350 (*LP*, IV, iii appendix 39).
17 B.L. Cotton MS, Titus B i fo. 274 (*LP*, IV, i 1267).
18 B.L. Cotton MS, Cleopatra F vi fos. 347–8 (Ellis, *Original Letters*, 3rd series, i. 360, 362–3; *LP*, IV, i 1266).
19 Hall, *Chronicle*, p. 699.
20 B.L. Cotton MS, Cleopatra F vi fo. 323 (*LP*, IV, iii appendix 36).
21 PRO SP1/34/fo. 164 (*LP*, IV, i 1295).
22 B.L. Cotton MS, Titus B i fo. 271–71^v (*LP*, IV, i 1272).
23 PRO SP1/34/fo. 192 (*LP*, IV, i 1321).
24 Coventry Record Office, A 79 i 55.
25 Hall, *Chronicle*, p. 696.
26 B.L. Cotton MS, Cleopatra F vi fo. 326^v (Ellis, *Original Letters*, 3rd series, ii. 7; *LP*, IV, i 1323).

ii. 7; *LP*, IV, i 1323).

27 Cf. Maddicott, *English peasantry*, p. 67; J. Campbell, 'England, Scotland and the hundred years war', in J. Hale, R. Highfield and B. Smalley, eds., *Europe in the late middle ages* (1965), p. 195.

28 *Cal. S.P., Spanish*, iii (i) no. 39 p. 86.

29 Hall, *Chronicle*, pp. 698–9.

30 PRO SP1/34/fo. 148 (*LP*, IV, i 1265); B.L. Cotton MS, Caligula E iii fo. 5 (badly damaged) (*LP*, IV, i 1261).

31 It would be unwise to argue from silence that there was no trouble elsewhere. In addition to the places that have been discussed in the text, there was also some resistance in Huntingdonshire where John Devereux, a gentleman, 'would not suffre the commissioners to sit'. On 9 May the king's attorney laid information against him and three others in star chamber: they had caused 'a greate and a right haynous ryott in maner of an Insurrection'. They confessed: Devereux was sent to the Tower, the others to the Fleet. On 19 May Devereux was led bare foot in his shirt to star chamber: he was then forgiven his offences, released from his fine and commanded to be of 'good abearing'. But it is impossible to say just when he had refused the Amicable Grant nor how large a protest it had been. (Hall, *Chronicle*, pp. 699, 701–2; BL, Lansdowne MS 639 fo. 58; Huntington Library, Ellesmere MS 2655 fo. 18; cited by J.A. Guy, *The Cardinal's Court* (Hassocks, 1977), pp. 74–5). It may be that unlawful assemblies alleged (on the same controlment roll as that listing those indicated in Suffolk) to have occurred at this time at Coventry and Leicester were connected with the Amicable Grant. About 75 men were named from Coventry and neighbouring places: they seem to have been summoned without effect on a number of occasions (PRO, KB 29/157 rot. xxvii^v–xxviii^r). About 280 men were named from Leicester and neighbouring places: they appeared and pleaded not guilty, a plea that was accepted by the king's attorney (PRO KB 29/157 rot. xxii^v–xxv^r. I owe my knowledge of this indictment to Miss Amanda Bevan.) Neither corresponds with any other sources; nor is there any corroborative evidence in KB 9 or KB 27 as far as I can trace. These may be riots wholly unconnected with the Amicable Grant: but it is worth keeping open the possibility that there were disturbances in parts of the country in addition to those known from the chroniclers and from commissioners' letters. I am very grateful to Mr S.J. Payling for sharing his knowledge of KB records with me. I refer to the Ellesmere MS by permission of the Huntington Library.

32 Dietz, *English Government Finance*, pp. 163–6; *LP*, XVII, 194, 280, 290, appendix 13; XIX, i 1032; ii 212, 328, 689; XX, i 85, 101, 984, 989; ii 211, 366, appendix 4 (2).

Note on Sources

The sources for the Amicable Grant are scanty: that makes this a medieval rather than a modern subject. Our sources begin with two chroniclers' accounts. Edward Hall's *Chronicle* was first published in 1548: the 1809 edition has been referred to here. Ellis Griffith's account survives in manuscript in the National Library of Wales, Aberystwyth (see T. Jones, 'A Welsh chronicler in Tudor England', *Welsh History Review*, i (1960), pp. 1–17): I have drawn on the translation from the Welsh of the part dealing with the Amicable Grant in *Historical Manuscripts Commission, Manuscripts in the Welsh language*, 48th appendix, part i, pp. ii–v. There are some two dozen letters to and from the king and Wolsey on the one hand, the commissioners for the Amicable Grant on the other. These have been printed in *Letters and Papers of Henry VIII*: in some cases the originals in the Public Record Office and the British Library do reveal significant variations or omissions. There are no council registers, except for some fragments in the Ellesmere MSS, Huntington Library, and in the Lansdowne MSS, British Library. There are very few local records, just some entries in the City of London records and a letter in Coventry Record Office. (I am most grateful to the many county and borough archivists who answered my inquiries about their collections.) We know what happened in London, Kent, East Anglia, Warwickshire; and also one or two other places on the basis of a single source. But we know nothing at all about what was happening in large parts of the country. There are indictments of rebels in East Anglia. But there are no interrogatories or depositions of the kind that illuminate the Lincolnshire rising of 1536. There were no articles of grievances. There are no newsletters, no books nor pamphlets, no contemporary reports of speeches, nothing like the accounts of the rebellions of 1549, other than the accounts by the chroniclers. What the historian of the Amicable Grant must therefore do is read and re-read the letters and the chronicles as sensitively as he can in order to wrest as much as possible from them.

Index

DATE DUE

IU 8014005 11-22-97			